Effective Law of Attraction

A Guide to Apply the Law of Attraction to

Improve Manifesting Power, and Manifest

the Income or Love You Deserve

Joe Silver

Copyright © 2020 All rights reserved.

The content contained within this book may not be reproduced, duplicated or transmitted without direct written permission from the author or the publisher.

Under no circumstances will any blame or legal responsibility be held against the publisher, or author, for any damages, reparation, or monetary loss due to the information contained within this book, either directly or indirectly.

Legal Notice:

This book is copyright protected. It is only for personal use. You cannot amend, distribute, sell, use, quote or paraphrase any part, or the content within this book, without the consent of the author or publisher.

Disclaimer Notice:

Please note the information contained within this document is for educational and entertainment purposes only. All effort has been executed to present accurate, up to date, reliable, complete information. No warranties of any kind are declared or implied. Readers acknowledge that the author is not engaged in the rendering of legal, financial, medical or professional advice. The content within this book has been derived from various sources. Please consult a licensed professional before attempting any techniques outlined in this book.

By reading this document, the reader agrees that under no circumstances is the author responsible for any losses, direct or indirect, that are incurred as a result of the use of the information contained within this document, including, but not limited to, errors, omissions, or inaccuracies.

Table of Contents

Introduction 5

    Are You Worthy of Success? 5

Section 1: The Laws 17

    Universal Laws 17

    The Law of Abundance 17

    The Laws of Quantum Physics 20

    The Law of Expectation 23

Section 2: Mind Models 25

    Trinity of Mind 25

    Brainwave Cycles 33

    Cognitive Behavior Triangle 38

    Be, Do, Have 40

Section 3: The Conditions 43

    Condition #1 Desire 46

    Condition #2 Thought 60

    Condition #3 Imagination 69

    Condition #4 Belief/Expectancy 79

    Condition #5 Feeling/Vibration 88

    Condition #6 Creative Attraction 99

    Condition #7 Inspired Action 106

    Condition #8 Manifestation 117

Section 4: The Qualities 123

    Quality #1 Attitude 124

    Quality #2 Awareness 125

Quality #3 Balance 127

Quality #4 Compassion 129

Quality #5 Confidence 130

Quality #6 Consistency 132

Quality #7 Charisma 134

Quality #8 Creativity 135

Quality #9 Flexibility 137

Quality #10 Focus 139

Quality #11 Forgiveness 142

Quality #12 Integrity 144

Quality #13 Motivation 149

Quality #14 Optimism 152

Quality #15 Patience 155

Quality #16 Responsibility 158

Section 5: Techniques to Raise Your Vibration 163

Technique #1 Goal Setting 163

Technique #3 Self-hypnosis 169

Technique #4 Meditation 172

Technique #5 Prepare to Receive 174

Technique #6 Gratitude 175

Technique #7 Practice Self-love 177

When it Doesn't Work 179

Create Your Law of Attraction Success Plan 180

Time is Now - Live it! 185

More Law of Attraction Resources 186

Introduction

Are You Worthy of Success?

Effective Law of Attraction is a book written for you to realize you are worthy of success.

I'm predicting you have a desire to completely fulfill the potential you came to this world with. You have a vision about how life could be, if you were empowered. You wish you could just get yourself to believe in the idea that you do have a say in how your life unfolds. You dream of a lifestyle which includes financial freedom and career success. You've often wondered if it's possible for you to enjoy deep, satisfying connections with people who love and support you. Of course, you hope to appreciate these things in a physical body that is the embodiment of good health.

But, let me make another prediction here. You're probably not experiencing life exactly on those terms right now.

Could it be that you are not worthy and deserving of the success you want?

There is nothing in this world that is too good for you. Your wanting to be successful is perfectly natural and healthy.

A desire for success is really your desire to enjoy a richer, fuller, and more abundant life.

To deny your desire for success is to deny your inherent nature. Within everyone's true nature is a longing to become all they can be, and you cannot help wanting to be all you can be.

To be all you can be requires many of nature's gifts.

Everything you see around you was placed here for you to experience, enjoy, taste, smell, touch, love, grow, and develop your fullest mental, spiritual, and physical self from.

You are worthy of living the life you imagine for yourself.

Putting it into the words from the soundtrack *The Greatest Showman* (which is hands down one of the most vibration raising movies I've ever seen):

This show, called your life, **IS** *the greatest show!*

> *"It's everything you ever want.*
>
> *It's everything you ever need.*
>
> *And it's here right in front of you.*
>
> *This is where you wanna be."*

Why would you settle for any less when you are capable of so much more?

We are often stifled by limiting beliefs, living in a state of negative thinking. It's easy to be completely unaware of how deeply it impacts us to live this way.

There is no benefit in focusing on lack. Yet, many people unconsciously make this choice every single day of their lives. They do not understand how damaging their conversations are, whether internal or external, and how this impacts their ability to manifest their desires, using the Law of Attraction.

The Law of Attraction may be working against you if you are focusing on lack and limitation, rather than abundance and freedom.

When applied correctly, the Law of Attraction allows you to live life freely, according to your deepest desires and enjoy unlimited access to all that is required for your highest mental, spiritual, and physical expression.

Effective Law of Attraction is a book which invites you to explore your true, unlimited potential and create an amazing life based on your heart's desire.

This book is for anyone who wishes to change their life for the better. However, you must be open to looking at old ways which haven't worked and learn how to implement new strategies to produce better results. This is true regardless of if you believe or do not believe in the Law of Attraction.

If you've been disillusioned or disenchanted because you did not get all you wanted within 30 days of trying Law of Attraction, then I believe you'll be relieved to understand that **Effective Law of Attraction** is distinct from any other book on this topic.

How you'll get the most value from this book is read it one time through to give yourself an overview. Practice the exercises as you come to each one.

By the time you have finished reading, you will understand exactly why you have failed to manifest what you want.

Then, you'll be ready to move beyond theory and begin applying real world action steps.

I've provided some suggested routines in the chapter, **Create Your Law of Attraction Success Plan**, to help you organize the exercises.

As you work through the exercises in each chapter, you'll align yourself with the conditions for manifesting. You'll be equipped with an instruction manual to create the life of your dreams.

Now, if you're someone who has experienced a lot of success already using Law of Attraction and want to move on to create bigger and more dramatic results in your life, then you will be able to advance your skills.

Finally, if you're a person who has never tried Law of Attraction and you're ready to do something different to experience more positive results in your life, I'm about to open your eyes to a whole new world and I love that.

My sincerest desire is for everyone to create a life that is in alignment with their highest self and their passion.

I can hardly wait to learn what you will manifest!

Who Am I?

Prior to becoming a Hypnotist, I used to be a stock broker.

I always knew I wanted to help people achieve their dreams.

I started meditating on this and visualizing a new future for myself.

After soul searching for some time, I stumbled upon a hypnotherapy training course.

Inside a few months, I became a Certified Hypnotherapist and opened my own office.

I was a stock broker by day, and by evening, I was writing scripts, recording meditations, and working on my website.

One afternoon, my branch manager called me into his office. There are few moments in one's life which are defining moments, when your life changes forever. Little did I know, I was about to experience one of them.

My bosses' words were, *"This is a conflict of interest. If you do not shut down this business immediately, then turn in your resignation."*

Right then and there, I was forced to make a decision which would impact my life.

Would I give up my hopes and dreams of my new hypnosis business?

Or would I risk everything, including a great income and forge ahead with my new plan?

Without a clue as to how I would survive, I cleaned out my office and walked out, my head held high.

I just knew I would figure out how I would make this business a success.

Yet, a few months later, my belief was severely put to the test, as I found myself in the hospital, needing lung surgery, and uninsured. The bill came to $30,000!

My ex-husband filed bankruptcy, leaving me with another $25,000 of debt.

I had startup costs for a business which, of course, was not yet generating any income.

Not surprisingly, my belief was getting outshined by heavy doses of reality crushing down upon me.

I blew through my entire savings.

This struggle went on for the next year and a half.

You see, the day I quit my job, I entered a fight or flight mode. I worked long hours and I told myself *"There was just not enough time in my day"* for personal development or meditating, the very things which initially helped me to pursue my dream.

Programming my mind for success, the very thing I was teaching other people to do, was low on my priority list.

A day came when I entered a deeply cathartic emotional breakdown, which was followed by a wake-up call.

The question came to my mind, *"Why am I choosing to create this? This is not I know!"* I immediately snapped out of this nearly 2-year inertia I had been living.

I had work to do to get my beliefs right again.

My meditation practice resumed immediately.

Shortly thereafter, inspirational ideas and insights were flooding my mind.

I was figuring out how to make a real living online with my hypnotic recordings, eBooks, and personal development courses.

Fast-forward to today, around 20 years later, my business has more than surpassed what I thought was even possible back then.

My passion has evolved somewhat over the years to include leading others through live trainings to achieve their desires and live the life of their dreams.

How I Define It

The Law of Attraction is not a new concept. It's always been around and it's constantly working, whether you believe in it or not. You can't get better at **using** the Law of Attraction because you're already using it. It already does work perfectly, 100% of the time. **Effective Law of Attraction** helps you get better at getting into alignment with the manifesting conditions, so you can manifest your heart's desire.

Perhaps you've heard it defined as *"ask, believe, and achieve,"* or some other 3-step process.

These featured steps are important elements to manifesting. However, it goes way deeper than that. What about action? When they say "believe," are they saying consciously or unconsciously?

Certainly, if you focus on those three steps, it's possible you might get results. However, if you are getting results focusing on only those three steps, then it's because you are unconsciously also applying some unmentioned steps.

If you haven't been getting results, then you'll understand why as we go through the manifesting conditions.

Here's How I Define Law of Attraction:

"Law of Attraction is when the manifesting conditions and personal qualities are developed and come into alignment simultaneously."

Law of Attraction is always working, either for you or against you. For most people who have never been introduced to some of the concepts discussed in this book, it's usually working against them.

It's an impersonal law. It's unbiased. In other words, it doesn't matter if what you think, imagine, feel, or believe is something you fear or something you desire, the law works the same exact way—always. It simply manifests whatever you are in alignment with.

Law of Attraction is not a quick fix. It is a way of life.

It's not a step by step formula or process, because you are starting *"the process"* from where you are right now, your own unique set of circumstances.

As you explore each of the manifesting conditions, you will gain a better understanding of how you have created the life situation, you're in now. You'll also learn the ways to stop creating more unwanted circumstances, and ultimately create a life you truly love.

How did Law of Attraction Originate?

The New Thought movement grew out of the teachings of Phineas Quimby in the early 19th Century. Early in his life, Quimby was diagnosed with tuberculosis. Unfortunately, medicinal treatment wasn't working.

In 1838, Quimby began studying Mesmerism. He became aware of the mental and placebo effect of the mind over the body when prescribed medicines of no physical value cured patients of diseases. From there, Phineas Quimby developed theories of mentally aided healing

It wasn't until 1877 that the term **"Law of Attraction"** first appeared in print, in a book which discusses esoteric mysteries of ancient theosophy, called **Isis Unveiled**, written by the Russian occultist, Helena Blavatsky, where she alluded to an attractive power existing between elements of spirit.

However, there have been many references even before the term was used, that describe what we understand today.

Gautama Buddha, (who lived between 563 BC - 480 BC): said *"What we are today comes from our thoughts of yesterday, and our present thoughts build our life of tomorrow: Our life is the creation of our mind."*

Empedocles (490 BC), an early Greek philosopher, hypothesized something called Love (philia) to explain the attraction of different forms of matter.

Plato alleged as early as (391 BC): *"Like tends towards like."*

The Bible has many statements suggesting the power of having faith and asking for what you want, such as: *"Ask, and it shall be given you; seek, and ye shall find; knock and it shall be opened unto you."*

By the 20th Century, a surge in interest in the subject led to many books being written about it, including:

The Science of Getting Rich (1910) by Wallace D. Wattles

The Master Key System (1912) Charles Haanel

How to Win Friends and Influence People (1936) Dale Carnegie

Think and Grow Rich (1937) Napoleon Hill

The Power of Positive Thinking (1952) Norman Vincent Peale

The Power of Your Subconscious Mind (1962) Joseph Murphy

Creative Visualization (1978) Shakti Gawain

You Can Heal Your Life (1980) Louise Hay

Law of Intention and Desire (1994) Deepak Chopra

How to Get What You Really, Really, Really, Really Want (1998) Wayne Dyer, public television special

The Secret (2006): The concept of the Law of Attraction gained a lot of renewed exposure with the release of the film and book written by Rhonda Byrne.

Since then, **Law of Attraction** became a bit more well-known. However, since the film represents the topic in a very basic manner with an inadequate basis for real-world application it contributes to some skepticism.

Things that Aren't True

Myth #1: The Law of Attraction Isn't True

It always surprises me how many bright, intelligent people there are who learn about Law of Attraction and flippantly write it off as nonsense. The only issue with Law of Attraction is one of misunderstanding of what it is and how it works.

Before you dismiss the Law of Attraction, ask yourself this: Would aligning your thoughts, feelings, beliefs, and behaviors with what you want help you or hinder you?

Here's the thing, a belief in the Law of Attraction is a belief in your ability to have control over deliberately creating your reality and manifesting whatever you desire.

The idea you have a say in how your life is going infuriates some people. I can only assume this is because they are receiving some counter intentions by remaining stuck in a belief system that supports them in maintaining a victim mentality.

If you are of the opinion that what you think and feel has no bearing on your reality, you will not be able to attract results that you desire.

The mind is set up in such a way that it favors information that conforms to your existing beliefs and discounts evidence that does not.

Remember, the Law of Attraction is always working. How it works for you is up to you.

Myth #2: The Law of Attraction Is Like a Genie Granting Your Every Wish

This is the myth which continues to perpetuate Myth #1, that it doesn't work. Since Law of Attraction does not actually work like a genie, those who go into it thinking all they need to do is make a wish and a magic genie will miraculously appear and grant their heart's desire are setting themselves up for disillusionment.

Approaching Law of Attraction, coming from this idea you can think yourself into receiving high-ticket items, like cars, dream homes, and lottery winnings, and change your life overnight, is unhealthy. It is the very reason why critics, skepticism, and misunderstanding about this Law exist.

While it's possible to achieve what you desire, it's going to require much more than thinking. It takes diligent effort to grow yourself into the person who is in alignment with your true desires.

Law of Attraction is common sense. It's a set of practical conditions the most successful people are naturally in alignment with. You need to have a clear desire and intention. Focus is required. You also need to be intentionally taking actions toward achieving what you want to create.

The more you align yourself with these conditions, the more the universal creative energy corresponds by sending you new ideas, intuitive messages, opportunities, helpful people, and other resources.

Myth #3: When Bad Stuff Happens, it is All Your Fault

No one knows exactly why catastrophic, horrible events happen to innocent, good, and well-intentioned people.

Some Law of Attraction advocates go too far and say you are responsible for every bad thing that's ever happened to you. There are no good answers to why terrible events happen to good people. I'm talking about the likes of getting raped, having your home burn down to the ground, or learning that you or a loved-one has been diagnosed with a terminal illness.

You certainly have every right to feel and process all the emotions you undergo when you experience a devastating loss or tragedy. One reason people remain stuck from moving on is they did not process their feelings. You can only heal what you feel.

The Law of Attraction is not about blaming you for everything that's ever happened to you in your life. Understand that sometimes bad things happen, like losing your job, going through a bad break-up, or not getting approved for your loan. Often enough, you can look back on those situations and see something better happened as a result, and it never would have happened had the bad thing never occurred.

What if, when bad things happened, you were to remain open to discovering how the event might play into a much grander, more intelligent plan that the universe has in store for you?

Here are a few other theories about why negative things might happen and how to deal with them when they do.

- The truth is, sometimes we do attract scenarios to ourselves by having fears about those things happening. Negative thoughts and energies do attract negative.
- If you believe in the concept that your soul has lived lives before this one, then you may be experiencing karma that originated several lifetimes ago.
- Again, if you believe in this idea that we have many lives and we create our lesson plans between lives, sometimes we orchestrate events we need to experience in this life for our soul to advance.
- It's completely random and we just don't have control over everything that happens to us. But we do have complete control over how we allow it to affect us as we navigate through our future.

The bottom line is, regardless of which scenario you subscribe to, it's tiresome and painful to try and pinpoint exactly why things happen to us. When life becomes difficult and painful, you have two options. 1) You can accept what happened; or 2) you can suffer.

Acceptance does not mean you are making the situation right or you like or want what happened. It simply means you have accepted the idea that no matter how much you dwell on it, you are not going to change what happened. Acceptance is a way of letting it go so you can make room for better things to happen.

One of the laws of nature is change or impermanence. The one constant is change. Everything and everyone will eventually die.

Make peace with the past. Accept it. Forgive it. Live in the present. Whatever happened, happened. Life is not always fair. If you are always focusing on how things were, and the injustice you feel, then you will continue to re-create your future from that state. No matter how bad it was, it is not happening now. It only exists in your memory. You do not have to let it control your thoughts, emotions, or bring it into your future.

Focus on what you have control over, which is how you choose to experience this present moment. Whatever you are focusing on, feeling, and imagining right now is what's creating your future.

Section 1: The Laws

Live your life as though your every act were to become a universal law.

- Immanuel Kant

Universal Laws

Universal Laws are guidelines that help us understand the rules we are playing by.

Everything in the world is made of energy and we are all connected with that energy.

Our thoughts, feelings, words, and actions are all forms of energy and is what creates our reality.

What's exciting about that is since our thoughts, feelings, words, and actions create the world around us, we have the power to create a world of peace, harmony, and abundance.

I've chosen to share just a few of those laws to help you understand how that is all possible.

The Law of Abundance

The Law of Abundance states that we live in an abundant universe. There is plenty of everything, including love, money, and all the necessities for everyone.

The key to having abundance is alignment with the conditions for manifesting it.

You likely grew up hearing things like *"there are starving children in Africa, so you need to eat every last bite of food that is on your plate."* Or *"money doesn't grow on trees."*

The truth is, there is abundance in the world. It is all around you. It's about what you are choosing to focus on. We don't have any issues with scarcity in the world, even when it comes to those starving children. The planet produces enough food. Hunger is not a problem caused by nature. Hunger is caused by lack of efficiency and politics.

I am illustrating how it does not serve any of us well to confuse issues like hunger, not to be ignored, with scarcity.

The Abundance Mindset

How you view the world can affect the opportunities you see, your beliefs, and ultimately your results. You can choose to see the world as a place of abundance or a place of scarcity.

An abundance mindset is hopeful, positive, and expects the best. It is also more altruistic, since you believe you'll receive what you need. It frees you up to do more for others.

A scarcity mindset, on the other hand, leads to negativity and selfishness. You feel the need to look out for yourself, even at the expense of others.

Abundance Mindset	Scarcity Mindset
There is plenty to go around. Everyone can win.	There is a limited supply of everything, and someone else must lose for you to win.
Life is easier. You believe anything is possible. Expect the best and things eventually go your way.	Life is difficult. Success is hard. You expect the worst and that's how it turns out.
Opportunities are easier to spot.	Opportunities are scarce, and you struggle to find them.
You take more risks. The bigger the risk, the bigger the reward.	You play it safe. You're afraid to lose.

| You are more relaxed. You enjoy life because all your needs are met. | You live in fear and pessimism. You must fight the world to get what you want and need. |

Which view do you normally see the world through? Abundance or scarcity?

One way to begin feeling the abundance, which may seem counter intuitive, is by giving more. Whatever resource you feel you lack, give that.

It feels good to give and it tricks you into believing you have plenty, which changes your energy and puts you into the flow of abundance.

How to Move from Scarcity to Abundance

1. **Focus on what you already have.** When you see that you already have enough, you feel abundant and are likely to attract more to you.
2. **Avoid people that complain a lot.** Complainers have a scarcity mindset. You're more susceptible to others' mindsets than you think. Spend time with positive people who have the mindset you want.
3. **Visualize an abundant future.** Instead of worrying about what you don't have, allow yourself to dream about what you want to achieve in the future.
4. **Keep a positive journal.** List the things in your life you feel grateful for. Be sure to mention all the people in your life. You probably have a home, a job, a car, family, friends, and so on. That's a good place to start.
5. **Be generous.** Demonstrate to yourself there is enough for everyone by sharing what you have, including time. The more you share, the more others want to reciprocate.

An abundance mindset won't magically put you into a Mercedes or add a few zeros to your bank account overnight. However, an abundance mindset will allow you to move forward with confidence as you take the necessary steps to make positive changes in your life.

The Laws of Quantum Physics

If you've been learning about Law of Attraction, you may have also heard the term Quantum Physics by now. Every day we are learning more information about this exciting topic.

What is Quantum Physics?

Quantum Physics is the study of the smallest particles of energy known to man.

According to the world of Quantum Physics, everything you see in the physical world at the most fundamental level comes down to one thing—energy!

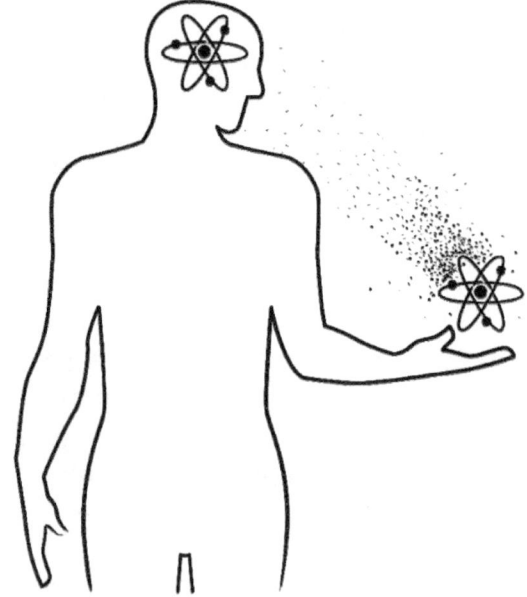

The Law of Attraction works based on the alignment of energy.

Nothing is solid, although many things you see around you appear so.

The energy of our thoughts is just as real as the energy of the physical things we see all around us. The difference between the energy of thoughts and the energy of physical things, is the rate with which the molecules are moving. Thought molecules move extremely fast. Molecules in physical objects move extremely slow, giving them that solid appearance. Look under a good microscope, you'll see, there's movement.

Fixate on a thought long enough. And it goes through a process of taking physical form. You daydream about it. You start believing in it. You get a feeling about it. And after a while, ideas to act come to you and eventually that thought has now become a thing.

While many things you see around you appear static, there is no such thing as stable. Everything is always in constant motion, it's either growing or decaying.

Think of this in terms of water. At a high rate of vibration, water is steam. You can barely see or feel steam. As the vibration slows and cools, it condenses into water, which we can perceive with our physical senses. Then, as it cools and slows further, it becomes apparently solid, ice. But, if you look very closely at the ice, it is still moving. It's freezing or melting.

Here's how Einstein states what I've explained:

> *"Everything is here and now, but in various states of visibility and invisibility depending upon the frequency that you are operating on, and that means the belief system, the definitions that you buy into most strongly."*

"Mass and energy are both but different manifestations of the same thing."

Everything you see and think about is energy.

Messages from Water

Masaru Emoto, Japanese author of *Messages from Water*, studied the effect human consciousness has on the molecular structure of water and revealed water does respond to our thoughts.

Emoto would expose water in glasses to positive and negative words, pictures, and music, then freeze them. Later, he examined the aesthetic properties of the resulting crystals with microscopic photography.

These studies found water exposed to positive speech and thoughts resulted in visually "pleasing" crystals. The negative intention would yield "ugly" frozen crystal formations.

Emoto said that this was because emotional *"energies"* and *"vibrations"* could change the physical structure of water.

Mirror Neurons

A mirror neuron is a neuron that fires both when an animal acts and when the animal observes the same action performed by another. The neuron "mirrors" the behavior of the other, as though the observer were itself acting.

Mirror neurons have also been detected in the human brain.

This is exciting. It means that certain behaviors, those which make the intention of the person obvious to the observer, activate the neurons in the observer's brain. This, in turn, causes the observer to be able to imitate the behavior.

So, as the person who is being observed, understanding how at a deep, unconscious level, the intentions you are sending out to others are being acted out in someone else's brain is something worth taking note of. It could even go so far as to be physically carried out and reflected to you.

The Law of Expectation

The Law of Expectation states whatever you expect with confidence and certainty becomes a self-fulfilling prophecy.

It's one of the most powerful laws in the universe. Whatever you expect becomes your reality.

Many people go through life thinking it should be hard. And since they expect it to be, it is. The universe gives them more of the same. It gives them a hard life filled with roadblocks and unforeseen challenges along the way. The expectation is delivered.

You can always change your expectation.

You can start expecting prosperity, abundance, happiness, adventure, thrills, and opportunity. What you expect is what you receive.

Something special happens when you change your expectation.

As soon as you make a choice to change your expectations, the universe jumps on board with you and helps you create what you expect.

You might think you expect something, but when you look at your actions you can tell what you are expecting.

The Placebo Effect

Scientists are determining the placebo effect is even more powerful and miraculous than previously thought.

Using new brain imaging techniques, they are discovering how a thought, belief, or desire creates biological changes in cells, tissues, and organs. Much of human perception is not based on information flowing into the brain from the outside world, rather what the brain expects to happen, based on previous experience.

A study was done in Japan on 13 people who were extremely allergic to poison ivy. Each had rubbed on one arm, a harmless leaf that they were told was poison ivy. On the other arm, they rubbed the actual poison ivy and were told it was harmless. All 13 broke out in a rash where the harmless leaf contacted their skin. Only two had reactions where the poison leaves were rubbed.

You will behave or act in a certain way because your behaviors are determined by the results you expect.

In other words, you will be motivated to take certain actions when you expect certain results.

When you expect success with absolute certainty, you take all the necessary actions to prepare for it.

To illustrate the power of positive - and negative - expectancy, Norman Vincent Peale tells the story of a group of people who, at the end of one year, committed to writing their expectations for the coming year. Each person sealed his expectations in an envelope to be opened and read aloud at the end of the following year.

At the end of the year the notes were opened; the expectations of each had been fulfilled. The man who had written "All I can expect is more of the old, miserable same," received in the New Year exactly what he had expected.

A woman who had listed 10 worthy goals she expected to achieve found that 9 of the 10 goals had been accomplished.

Another man, basing his expectations upon the negative outlook for his Capricorn birth sign, predicted, "I look for difficulties and frustrations." His negative expectations were realized. A woman in the group, whose birth sign was the same, did not know she should expect difficulties and predicted a satisfying year, which had indeed come to pass.

Another man in the group had written, "As none of the men in my family have survived beyond the age of 60, therefore, I expect to die this year." The man's death occurred one month before his sixtieth birthday. Each of us receives exactly what we expect, whether our expectations are positive or negative. We can see from these examples and from the many we have met during our lives that an attitude of positive expectancy is crucial to accomplishment and personal success.

Section 2: Mind Models

The key to growth is the introduction of higher dimension of consciousness into our awareness.

- Lao Tzu

Trinity of Mind

Law of Attraction is a collaboration between the conscious, subconscious, and superconscious mind.

It's a collaboration between thoughts, feelings, and actions.

It's a collaboration between body, mind, and spirit.

When we speak of mind, we usually think of the brain.

The mind is not the brain. The mind is unseen, unphysical. It uses the physical brain, but it's not contained there. The mind is everywhere, including each cell of your body.

Your mind is broken down into three distinct parts, each playing an important role in your life.

- The conscious mind
- The subconscious mind
- The superconscious mind

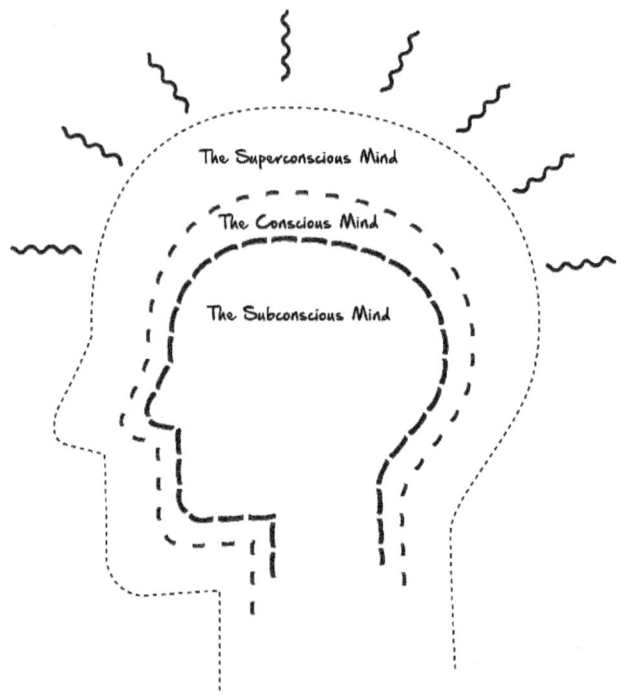

Your conscious and subconscious mind are unique and personal to you, whereas the superconscious mind is impersonal and connects all the minds in the universe.

Let's start with the conscious and subconscious mind, then we'll explore the superconscious.

According to cognitive neuroscientists, 5% of your mind is conscious awareness, the remaining 95% is subconscious. We do not know the exact percentage for certain.

Your subconscious mind is more powerful than anyone can comprehend. It influences most of your conscious thoughts and behaviors.

Conscious Mind

The conscious mind is working right now as you read this. It is the part of you fully aware of what is going on right now. Choices and decisions are made by the conscious mind.

Functions of the Conscious Mind

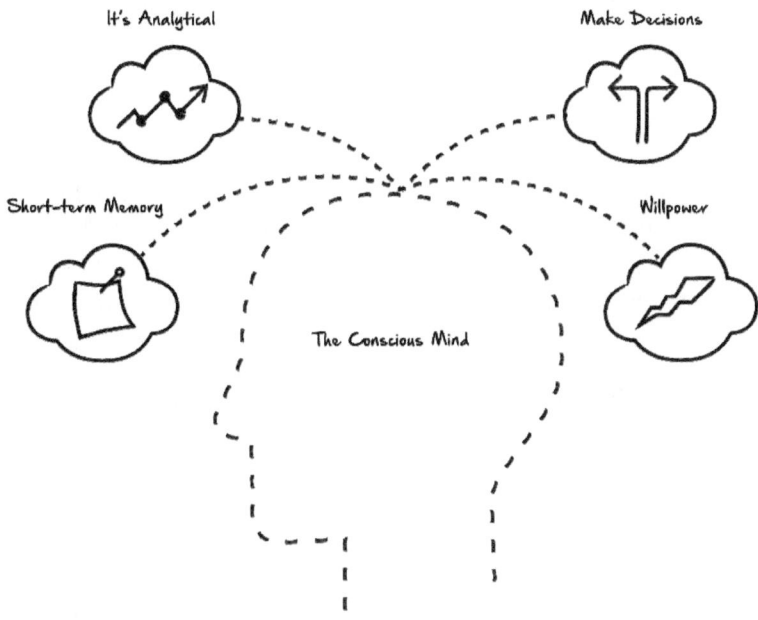

- **Short-term Memory** – This is the memory we refer to throughout the day as we function. You use this when making your to do list and remembering your appointments.
- **It's Analytical**– It can evaluate facts and data, it solves math problems, and helps you with spelling.

- **Makes Decisions** – Should I call them? Should I buy this? What am I going to wear?
- **Willpower** – Today I will eat healthy. Just one more push up. I will get up on time.

A special note on willpower is that it is only there to get you through the short-term. You will usually fail at making permanent changes by willpower alone because it's completely overpowered by your subconscious programming.

Subconscious Mind

The subconscious mind controls all your habits and emotions. The subconscious mind can be compared to a computer that stores the data for all the experiences you've ever had. It is unlike the conscious in that it does not analyze or rationalize. You are communicating with the subconscious mind when you dream.

Functions of the Subconscious Mind

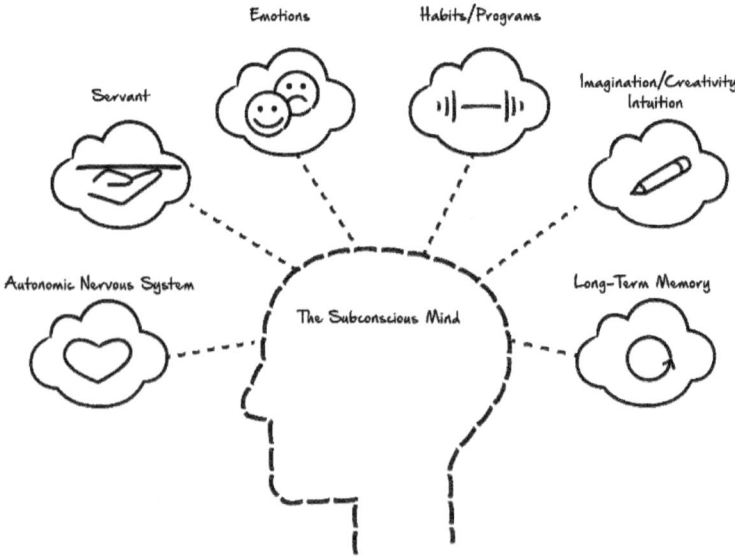

- **Autonomic Nervous System** — The ANS affects heart rate, digestion, respiration, pupils, arousal, and virtually every automatic function of the body.
- **Servant** — The subconscious mind will do whatever we command it to do. The only limits are those we assign to it based on what we think is possible.
- **Emotions** — When you feel anxiety, anger, or fear, these experiences are at the subconscious level of mind. Love, happiness and peace is also generated by chemical responses within your subconscious mind.
- **Habits/Programs** — We develop our programs and habits through experiencing daily life; also, through repetition. An example of a program is learning to drive. When you first learned to drive, you had to be extremely aware. Now that you have driven thousands of times, it is ingrained in your subconscious mind and you don't even think about it anymore.
- **Imagination/Creativity/Intuition** — When you get an extraordinary thought, a new idea, a hunch about something, you are in touch with the creative part of your subconscious mind.
- **Long-Term Memory** — Our subconscious mind stores every experience you have ever had. It remembers everything about your entire life history. Even old, forgotten memories, still reside at the subconscious and may even be influencing your thoughts and behaviors to this very day!

There is one other part of the mind to make special note of here called *the critical factor*.

Critical Factor

To put it simply, it prevents you and protects you from haphazardly making wildly dramatic changes within your subconscious mind.

The key to changing the subconscious programming is getting past the pearly gates of the good ole critical factor, and this can be awfully tricky!

The best way is by getting the mind into a very relaxed, yet aware state, where you are sweet-talking the gatekeeper to let you pass.

Later in the chapter on Self-hypnosis, we'll discuss the technique in more detail.

Superconscious Mind

The superconscious mind has been referred to as the collective conscious or infinite intelligence.

You've heard of the sixth sense before. If you've ever experienced that phenomenon where you get that gut instinct, you've been touched by the superconscious mind. Suddenly you receive a flash of inspiration, an idea, or a hunch. That is the communication which comes from the superconscious mind.

The superconscious mind is where all creative imagination and intuitive guidance exists.

Every mind on the planet is connected at this level of mind. It is the source of all knowledge.

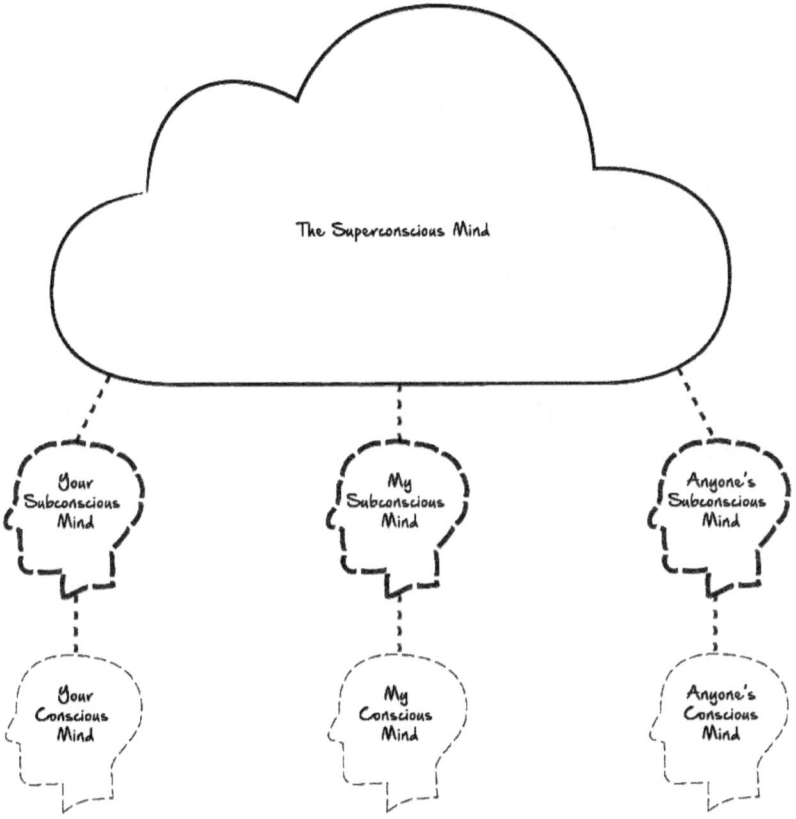

The very best ideas ever created came from the superconscious mind. Every great inventor, genius, or artist either knowingly or unknowingly taps into this intelligence to solve any problem they are working on.

Your connection to the superconscious mind, is through the subconscious mind.

Here's an example of how it works:

You might be in self-hypnosis, visualizing with strong emotion about your desire.

Not every thought is strong enough to enter the realm of the superconscious.

Mere words, which have no emotion, just wont do.

Only clear thoughts, which are highly charged with emotions can enter the realm of the superconscious.

Now, in what would appear to be an entirely unrelated situation, there's some other person out there in this vast universe, who has had a thought at one time or another, which just so happens to BE the perfect idea you need to act on. This thought is out there at the superconscious level.

At some point later, you receive an idea, seemingly out of the blue, which you feel the urge to act upon. That is the superconscious way of communicating with you.

Now you need to act. That is how you will strengthen your connection with the superconscious.

Brainwave Cycles

Whether you're deeply asleep or fully awake, your brain is busy with activity. Your brain is a buzz with millions of little messengers, called electrical neurons which are sending signals back and forth, which contain important information.

Some of these signals tend to repeat frequently and so brainwave patterns are formed.

In neuroscience, there are five distinct brain wave frequencies, namely Beta, Alpha, Theta, Delta and the lesser known Gamma.

Understanding how your brainwaves function allows you to use your brain more effectively. It also helps to distinguish the qualities of each state, so you can enter the best level of brainwave frequency that will facilitate the experience you want.

Beta

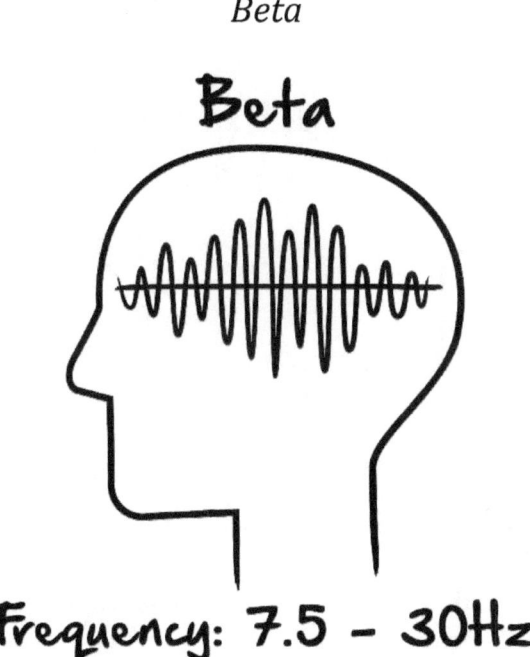

Conscious Mind – Awake - Alert – Optimal state for focus, goal setting, creating affirmations

Frequency: 12 - 30Hz

Beta brainwaves are the second fastest and highest frequency brainwaves. They occur when we are fully conscious, aware, and focused.

You're in a beta state when you are in a state of increased alertness. This may include times when you are having an active conversation, playing sports, giving a presentation, or interviewing for a job. When you are at a beta level, you experience your mind being very sharp. You're able to think fast and act decisively. Beta waves stimulate concentration and problem-solving ability.

Alpha

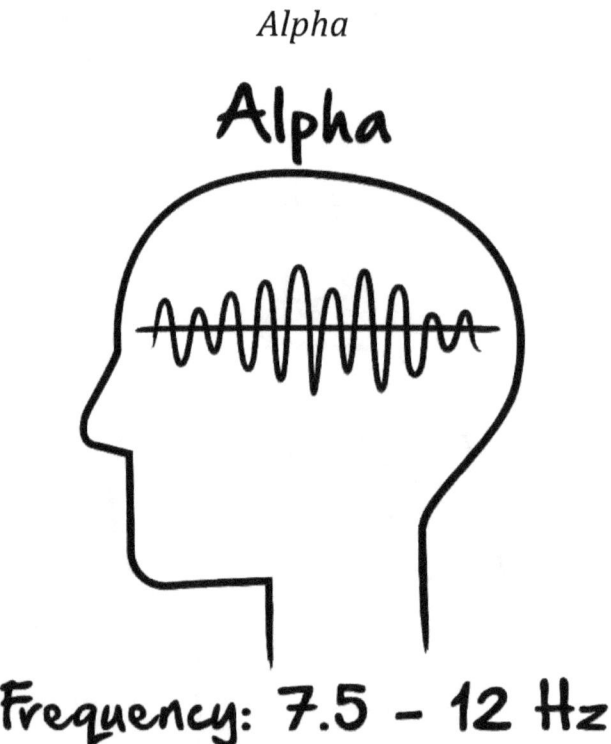

Gateway to the subconscious mind: Optimal state for visualization, meditation, and repeating affirmations

Frequency: 7.5 – 12 Hz

Alpha brainwaves are a bit slower, bringing about feelings of calm, relaxation, and well-being. At this state, you are semi-conscious. You're not sleeping, but you're also not very attentive to your environment. You can think of this state as those times when your mind is elsewhere, like when you start to zone out and daydream. You may even notice answers to problems may occur to you during this time.

Being in the alpha state is a pleasant, almost euphoric feeling. Because your mind is relaxed, it's a helpful and easy state you'll almost automatically access, whenever you are meditating or visualizing.

Theta

Subconscious mind –- Light sleep: Optimal state for meditation and hypnosis

Frequency: 4 - 7.5 Hz

Theta is an elusive, very DEEP and slow brainwave state, which is somewhere between that point when you are so relaxed, almost asleep, but not quite.

With theta brainwaves, you can access a profound state of meditation or contemplation.

You may see vivid imagery while in theta and you might even feel like you are floating away from consciousness.

Theta waves can enhance creativity, reduce stress, awaken your intuition, and even help you develop your extrasensory perception. Some of the best ideas may come to you when you are relaxing here.

When entering this slower and deeper theta frequency state, your mind has disengaged from your logical and aware conscious mind. It becomes very creative and imaginative.

You are also most receptive to suggestions in theta, and therefore, they will more easily enter your subconscious mind.

If the theta state of mind helped **Albert Einstein** tap into his own inner brilliance, just IMAGINE what it could do for you!

The possibilities are limitless.

Delta

Unconscious – Access to Superconscious – Sleep. Optimal state for sleeping and restoring your physical body.

0.1 – 4 Hz

Delta waves are the slowest, lowest frequency. Anything slower than that and well ... you don't want to know.

It's extremely hard to stay conscious in this state, therefore you may enter a state that is beyond your consciousness.

This brainwave pattern has been detected in deeper meditative states and some say it may be a portal to the realm of the superconscious.

Delta waves naturally occur during deep, dreamless sleep. Some people claim you can access the delta state while still consciously aware.

One of the many reasons sleep is so important is because when these slower brainwave frequencies are emitted, and you experience complete loss of awareness, these frequencies have a restorative and healing effect on the physical body and revitalize your brain.

Gamma

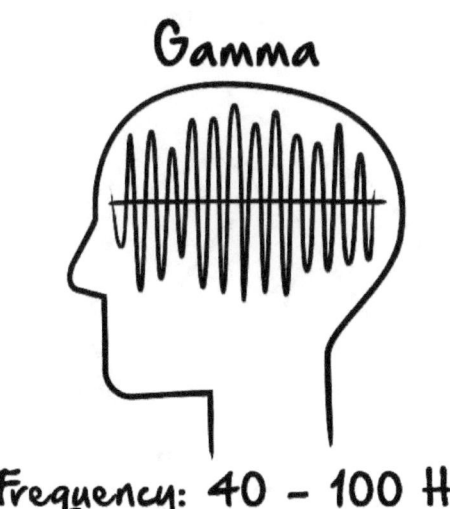

Ultra-Consciousness – Bliss State - Access to Superconscious

40 - 100 Hz

Gamma waves are typically experienced by the most practiced meditators, such as nuns or monks. They're also linked to peak mental and physical states athletes experience when they're *"in the zone."*

Any way that you get to this state, they are a sacred feeling and a shift in your overall state of consciousness

You are feeling pure bliss, ecstasy, joy for life, love, and compassion. Think of an intensely divine orgasm, that felt spiritual. That is a gamma brain wave experience.

Neuroscientists say you can produce more gamma brainwaves by focusing on feeling love and compassion. It certainly won't hurt you one bit to start focusing more on those feelings, would it?

Cognitive Behavior Triangle

Did you ever wonder why it's so hard to break a bad habit? Here's one reason.

Your thoughts, feelings, and behaviors are all part of a cycle which are connected. One part of the cycle effects the other.

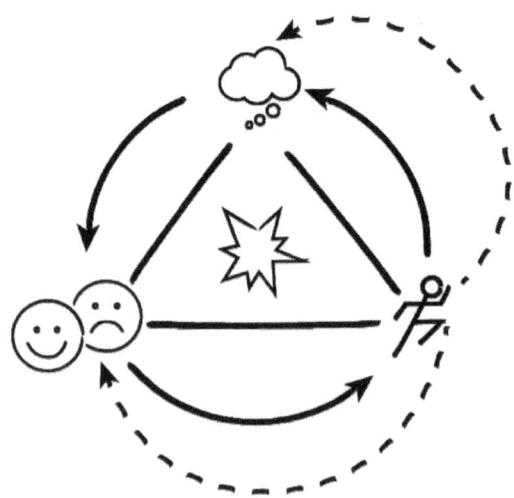

Here's how it works:

An event happens...

You THINK (X)

Which Makes you FEEL (Y)

And Makes you ACT (Z)

The ACT (Z), then reinforces your thoughts (X) and you Feel (Y)

This automatic cycle is designed to make your life easier.

Except when your thoughts are counterproductive to what you want to experience.

Your brain houses a vast network of about 100 billion neurons. Neurons are passing signals to each other, via as many as 1,000 trillion synaptic connections. These signals are how you automatically remember to press the brake pedal when you come to a red light. It's instant. You don't have to think about it.

At the level of your neural network, a signal is passed from one neuron that represents the red light, to another neuron which signifies stop, by way of chemicals, known as neurotransmitters.

The more often the message gets sent back and forth between these neurons, the more deeply ingrained that association becomes.

This can be positive, and in cases where you are trying to break a habit or form a new habit, it can become a very negative thing.

For example:

For this case, we'll use your alarm clock going off as the event.

If, when you're alarm goes off, you think, *"I'm so tired, I don't want to get up yet."*

That thought is going to cause you to experience this feeling of being tired.

This feeling will most likely result in pushing the snooze button.

Each time you press the snooze button (take that action) you are reinforcing this behavior. At the neural level, you are literally connecting the event of the alarm going off with the action of pressing the snooze button every time you do it.

So, how do you change this?

You must intervene between what you think and the resulting action.

If you were to think in a new positive way, such as, *"I love getting out of bed," "I'm ready to start my day,"* or *"I have lots of exciting things to accomplish today, let's go!"* Those thoughts cause you to experience a new feeling, such as motivated.

When you feel motivated, you're more inclined to get out of bed, rather than pressing snooze.

Over time, the neural network learns the new behavior and it becomes the new automatic behavior.

As you simply become more aware of what thoughts are triggering the result, you can change those thoughts, which change your feelings. Your actions will change and so will your results.

Be, Do, Have

I want to share a model for life which will support you in attracting everything you want to attract with Law of Attraction.

I'm talking about flipping the switch on the most common approach to life.

You see, many people go through life with an approach that goes something like this:

If I DO this, then I will HAVE that, and then I will BE.

Example: If I work hard, then I will have lots of money, and then I will be happy.

Or, another approach people have is:

When I HAVE this, then I will DO that, and then I will BE.

When I have more energy, then I will go to the gym, then I will be confident.

In both approaches, your BEING is depending on something external to you, a future circumstance, which you feel must be in place for you to feel a certain way.

You're choosing not to experience the state of being you want.

The dilemma with this approach to life is this...

You can never BE anything because of an outer circumstance.

Once you do HAVE the money, the money isn't going to make you BE happy. You may experience temporary pleasure or satisfaction but money, in and of itself, can never make you be permanently happy.

Now, here's the truth about states of being. Whether it's happy, successful, peaceful, love, confident, or whatever other state you think having your desires fulfilled is going to make you feel, you don't require those things first in order to experience those states of being. You have access to those states right now. Nothing else external needs to take place for you to be happy. You can choose it right now.

What's important to understand about this is the very essence of what Law of Attraction is about. Law of Attraction and the results you want to produce from it are attracted to who you are, your beingness. So, if you are waiting to be something before you get something, you're going to be waiting a pretty long time. The sooner you can get yourself to experience the state of being you think the fulfillment of your desires will magically put into you, the sooner you can have your desires.

Be, Do, Have is an approach to life that puts you more in control of your life and how you perceive it.

You must BE. Then you will DO. And then you will HAVE.

Begin now, being the person, you dream of being. Do the things that person does. Eventually, you will have everything that is in alignment with who you are being.

If you want to attract abundance into your life, for example, experience the feeling abundance brings. Be happy, be peaceful, be content. From that beingness, you do. You take the actions necessary from the state of abundance. Naturally, you draw in the resources for and eventually the outcome you desired to have in the first place.

This model works the same no matter what it is you are trying to attract into your life, be it love, money, or health.

This is a paradigm shift that needs to take place before you can ever manifest the life of your dreams.

Section 3: The Conditions

Within all of us is a divine capacity to manifest and attract all that we need and desire.

- Wayne Dyer

The 8 Conditions of Manifesting

How to begin the *process* of manifesting.

In the previous sections, I described the context for which Law of Attraction exists.

Now, the **how to** will be given.

Step 1:

You've discovered this fantastic idea called the **Law of Attraction** which promises *"all of your dreams can become a reality.* "Everything is getting more exciting. You perform a basic Google search for *"how to manifest"* or some similar search term. What do you find? Approximately 200 million results! The most common formula presented is one coined from popular books and the movie, **The Secret**, all which suggest there are 3 simple steps to the Law of Attraction.

There are countless listings that suggest you can use *"7 steps to manifest anything you want"*—or maybe 5 or 4. Perhaps, you'll see *"how to manifest overnight"* or *"manifest instantly."* The options go on...and on. The list of formulas, processes, systems, step-by-step strategies is endless. Each promotes a similar thinking strategy, *"follow these steps in this particular order, and all your dreams will come true."*

Step 2:

Figure out which one of these approaches makes the most sense for you and start following each step.

Step 3:

After anywhere from 1-to-7 days, to even God forbid, 30 days or more trying to manifest what you want, you find yourself in a dilemma. There you sit, still trying to manifest what you want. Now you're thinking, *"yup, just like I thought all along, the Law of Attraction doesn't work!"* Sound familiar?

Yet, somewhere deep inside you, you still long to believe. This stuff is out there for a reason so being resilient, you get up, dust yourself off, and try again—even harder this time. And again, you fail to get the results you want! Now you have double the data and double the discouragement.

What happened?

Here's the deal. While each of these approaches have some truth to them, the strategy is somewhat flawed, when presented as a linear step-by-step process.

The Law of Attraction is not a step-by-step, one-size-fits all process and it's not linear.

A linear process is something that progresses directly from one stage to another with a starting point and an ending point.

LOA is most often described as a process because it's easier to explain and market the concept that way.

I'm willing to risk going against all those other processes to share the truth from my experience. The Law of Attraction is a bit messier than what's popularly suggested and if you want to make it work, I suggest following good old Einstein's wise words, *"If you want different results, you have to try different approaches."*

My experiences show that manifesting is best described in non-linear terms. I say, it does not progress or advance like phases, going in some logical sequence. Rather, "Law of Attraction is when the *manifesting conditions* and *personal qualities* are *developed* and come into *alignment simultaneously.*"

Each condition plays an important role in manifesting. And they do not always happen in the order in which they will appear in this section. These conditions can all be in play at once.

Law of Attraction is about being in alignment with all eight of the manifesting conditions, simultaneously.

The *"formula,"* if you will, is to simply work through each of the conditions for manifesting. By doing this you will gain an understanding of what it means to be in alignment with that condition. Be sure to do the exercise assignments to further support your endeavor.

Think of it a little like juggling 8 balls at a time. Start by getting good at juggling the one ball. Then add a second, and a third. With practice, soon you will learn to juggle all 8 balls at once. This is when you are in alignment with your manifestation.

The time it takes is the time it takes. Seriously! You can be in alignment with all 8 conditions within a matter of a second or it can take 20 years. It all depends on how quickly or slowly you get into alignment with each condition. But the moment you are in alignment, manifestation is instant.

The Manifesting Conditions:

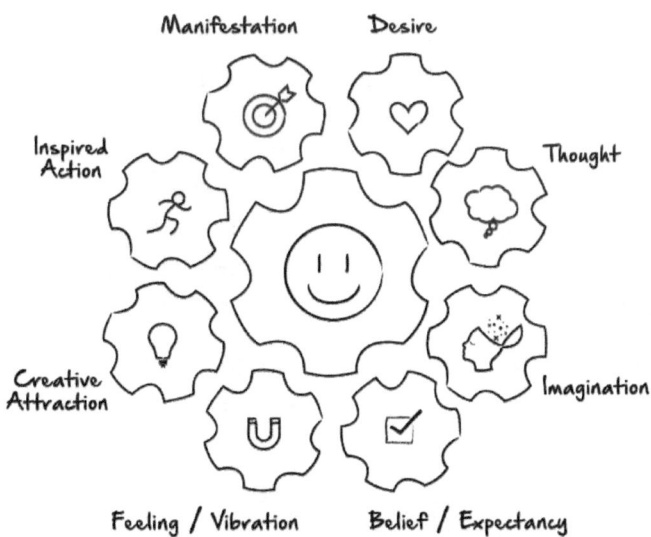

"Law of Attraction is when the manifesting conditions and personal qualities are developed and come into alignment simultaneously."

Condition #1 Desire

Defined: A strong feeling of wanting to have something or wishing for something to happen.

"The starting point of all achievement is desire."

- Napoleon Hill

Where do we begin?

We are going to start with what would seem to be the most likely beginning, which is desire and end with what would seem to be the end, manifestation.

Desire gets a bad rap sometimes in the *"spiritual"* community.

According to the religion Buddhism, *"Desire is the root of all suffering."* It suggests we should try to eliminate our desires.

Let's speak to this.

Desire is good, in and of itself, so long as that desire is pure. Desire, itself, is not what causes suffering. Desire is what causes you to expand and become bigger and better than the day before. Desire is a natural and universal impulse toward action.

You will always have desires. It's in your true nature as a human being, created by a creator who had the desire to create you in the likeness of himself, in the first place.

Desires, just like the universe, are infinite. Even after you fulfill one desire, a new desire is born.

Our cumulated desires cause this whole universe to expand.

So, you need to make peace with desire.

Where it becomes a problem and does create suffering is when we are *attached* to our desire. When we are attached to our desire, it's because we fear our desire won't be fulfilled.

In the Seven Spiritual Laws of Success, Deepak Chopra states:

> *"Inherent in every intention and desire is the mechanics for its fulfillment ... intention and desire in the field of pure potentiality have infinite organizing power.*
>
> *And when we introduce an intention in the fertile ground of pure potentiality, we put this infinite organizing power to work for us."*

You could not have a desire if you were not meant to achieve that desire. It literally could not be born within you unless you were meant to have it. If you desire anything, it is meant to be yours. The only thing keeping you from having it is your thoughts.

Think about this, everything you now enjoy about your life right now is the by-product of someone's desire. You're here, enjoying (hopefully) the very words on this page. For that to happen, I once had a desire to write a book and have it published so that people like you could benefit from it.

All that went into the process of this book getting into your hands was the by-product of many people's various desires. The computer I used to write the book. The website, where you bought the book. The bookstore. Someone had a desire to create a money holder; your wallet, which holds your credit cards.

The couch, chair, or bed where you are sitting or lying down was once a desire someone had. They wanted to invent this and then went into the business to create it.

As a matter of fact, everything including you, yourself, was sourced from someone's desire. Your mother and father most likely had a desire for a baby and out of their desire for that, or their love or attraction to each other, you were born.

Desire is fundamental and is at the heart of your actions.

Again, desire in and of itself is necessary. It is crucial if you're going to manifest anything.

Where does desire come from?

Pure desire originates from within. It hasn't been tainted or tampered with by our logical and rational thoughts.

Pure desire may even seem irrational to your logical mind and to everyone else with whom you might share your real desire.

Desire that is pure comes from your spirit and is felt through your heart. That is why it's called *"your heart's desire."*

Desire that comes from your mind, your thoughts, is still a desire, just not the true essence of your desire. It comes from what you have learned throughout your whole life, what you think you should have, do, or be. It comes from wanting the opposite of what you are experiencing. It's not wrong. It just may be slightly altered from your true desire.

The Complaint Game

What is a complaint? It's a statement that a situation is unsatisfactory or unacceptable.

Complaining, when it comes to the Law of Attraction is: The state of experiencing something you don't like.

When you complain about something, you are sending negative energy into the universe and asking it to bring you more of the experiences you don't like.

For example:

When you say:	What the universe hears:
My clients are always late.	Make my clients late more often.
I have so many bills to pay.	Give me more bills.
The restaurant always messes up my order	Keep messing up my orders, even more
I hate sitting in traffic.	Bring on even more traffic!

While complaining, you are giving attention to the idea in your sentence. *Clients Late. Bills to Pay. Messed up Order. Traffic*

You can just as easily say.

Instead of saying:	Say
My clients are always late.	I like my clients to show up on time.
I have so many bills to pay.	I enjoy having more money left over.
The restaurant always messes up my order	I love it when my order comes out perfectly
I hate sitting in traffic.	I love a smooth and easy drive!

Your complaints can also be a helpful tool in getting you back into alignment with your heart's desire.

It's easier to get in touch with what you don't like than it is to be aware of what you do like.

Knowing what you do like will help guide you toward your pure desire.

Exercise 1: The Complaint Game

Time: 5 minutes
Worksheet Available: Complaint Game

Download your worksheet at:
http://www.victoriamgallagher.com/ploabook

People love to complain.

Choose a personal issue or area of your life where you are currently unsatisfied.

- Love/relationships
- Career/success/money
- Health

You are going to take 5 minutes to complain about everything that makes you unhappy in this area of your life.

This exercise can be done solo, or you can grab a buddy and ask them to play the therapist role.

If doing it solo, you will simply make a list of a minimum of 10 complaints you have in this area.

If doing it as a pair, one person will play the role of client. The other person will play the role of therapist. The person playing therapist will simply listen to you and scribe everything you are saying and prompt you to continue for 5 minutes. They do nothing other than listen attentively and take notes. Although, if there is silence, the therapist will ask: What else bothers you?

As a client, you will complain to the therapist for about 5 minutes. To further illustrate this, I've included a couple of examples.

Allow me to introduce a couple of my volunteers, who will assist us in demonstrating the exercises throughout this book.

Emma the Entrepreneur

Emma is a 40-year-old Life Coach/Internet Marketer who was frustrated she wasn't creating a life of freedom, nor a stable, growing income stream from her client base since she left her corporate job 5 years ago.

After diligently working through the manifesting conditions, Emma was eventually able to attract a steady stream of new and higher paying clients who constantly refer her new business. She now enjoys the lifestyle of freedom she aspired toward.

Emma's Complaints:

1. Its hard to find new clients.

2. My bank account is always low.
3. My clients show up late
4. I have to spend too much time marketing.
5. I have no personal life.
6. I'm tired.
7. I'm stressed.

Soulmate Seeker Sam

Sam is a 53-year old man, who was single for 6 years after losing the love of his life. He was lonely and desperate to find love. He grew so discouraged by the women he was meeting that he was about to give up on ever finding the one he was meant to spend his life with.

A friend of his gave him this book and though he was reluctant, he was willing to try anything. He began to diligently work his way through each of the chapters. Within only 3 months, he met his soulmate, Sally, and they married a year later.

Sam's Complaints

1. It's hard to find interesting people.
2. I don't have a connection with anyone.
3. There is no one for me.
4. Why did she die.
5. I'm bored.
6. I'm sad
7. I'm stressed.

Now it's Your Turn:

Exercise 2: Discover Your Preferences

Time: 10 minutes
Worksheet Available: Discover Your Preferences
Download your worksheet at:http://www.VictoriaMGallagher.com/ploabook

Change the complaint to a preference.

Look at each of the complaints you wrote down and convert them into an opposite and positive counter statement.

Express exactly what situations you'd prefer to experience instead.

The point of your preferences is to change the focus from something you don't like or are complaining about to focusing on the idea that you want to replace it with instead; your preference.

Your preference statements will help you clarify and get specific about your desire.

For example, if you wrote down:

"It's hard to find new clients"

That would become:

"I love it when finding clients comes easily."

Notice I did not say, *"Finding clients is easy"* because that's not true for this case, is it?

It needs to be true and believable.

If you write statements that are not believable, say for instance; "I am a millionaire." What's happening in your mind when you say that? You're resisting it. You're rejecting it. It makes you feel bad. It defeats the purpose to lie to yourself, because lying makes you feel bad. In a moment, I'm going to give you some sentence starters which help you to create preferences that you can more easily buy into.

But first, let's go over a few more points.

It needs to specifically address the complaint.

The reason we started with your complaints is to give you some insight into your limiting beliefs that are holding you back from your desire. Therefore, to acknowledge each complaint specifically, your preference statements need to powerfully answer and redefine your view in this area. So, be sure that your statement creates a new perspective on your old way of thinking about it.

It needs to be stated in a positive way.

Here we are learning how to focus on what you do want to manifest instead.

For example, if one of your complaints was, "It's hard to find new clients." You wouldn't say: "It's not hard to find new clients." Because you're still focusing on the key word that it's hard. Instead you would say: I love it when finding clients comes easy.

It needs to feel good.

When coming up with your preference statements, make them feel as good as possible by adding in even more specifics:

Your original preference statement was:

"I love it when finding clients comes easily."

Ask: What would feel even better?

Your new answer might be:

"I love working with an abundance of my ideal clients."

Then Ask: What would be even better than that?

"I love being paid generously by an abundance of my ideal clients."

We took a complaint: "It's hard to find new clients," which is negative and feels bad, and turned it into a preference: "I love being paid generously by an abundance of my ideal clients, which is positive and feels good. It's believable and it's specific.

You'll continue repeating this process until you've addressed each complaint on your list.

Many times, people will try to simply change the sentence by saying they don't or won't do the thing they complained about.

For example; if one of your complaints was, "My bank account is always low," you might be tempted to say, "My bank account is not low anymore ..."

To change this phrase to a preference, you would state, "I prefer to see an abundance in my bank account."

A good rule of thumb is to make sure your sentences do not include any of the following negative words or phrases:

Not, Don't, Wont, No, Can't, Never, Avoid, Give Up, Ignore, No Longer, Refuse, Stop, Quit, Try, But, Hope

To help you to form sentences that are believable and positive, here are some sentence starters.

I enjoy ...

I choose to ...

I am working toward ...

I now create ...

I look forward to …

I am in the process of …

I am committed to …

I like …

I love it when …

It feels good when …

I prefer …

I can …

I am willing to …

I am learning to …

I am practicing …

I am choosing to believe …

I choose to feel …

Every day in every way, I feel myself attracting …

I'm open to receiving …

Emma's Preferences:

1. I love it when finding clients comes easy
2. I prefer to see an abundance in my bank account
3. It's great when my clients show up on time.
4. I'm finding ways to be more efficient with my time spent on marketing.
5. I choose to make more time for myself.
6. I am getting plenty of rest and becoming energized.
7. I make time to relax and unwind.

Sam's Preferences:

1. There are lots of interesting people in this world.
2. I begin by connecting with myself

3. The right person is out there for me.
4. I accept what happened and move forward.
5. I'm lucky to have time to find new ways to enjoy myself.
6. I embrace all my feelings. They're all important.
7. I'm changing my perspective and feeling more relaxed.

Now it's your turn:

Exercise 3: Get Clear on Your Desire

Time: 10 minutes
Worksheet: Discover Your Preferences

Once you have gone through all the complaints, and written out approximately 10 preferences, read through each of your preference statements. From this list, choose the words and phrases from each of your preferences that feel best to you and draw a circle around them.

This is getting laser clarity, the kind of clarity that allows everyone and everything around you to deliver exactly what you want.

Draw a circle around the words and phrases that make you feel good. You'll be using these words to create your Desire and Y Statement.

Exercise 4: Desire, Intention, and Gratitude Statement

Time: 20 Minutes
Worksheet Available: Desire and Intention Statement
www.VictoriaMGallagher.com/ploabook

Step 1: Desire Statement: Look at the preference words and phrases you circled in Exercise #3: Get Clear on Your Desire.

Now, let's get even more clear on that preference as it relates to your desire in life.

Using the preference words and phrases you circled, clearly write out your major desire. What does your idea of success look like for you in this area? There are no limits, only perceived limits. Everything is possible; nothing is impossible. Your desire needs to mean something to you and hit you emotionally. Why is this important to you?

Step 2: Intention Statement: Next, clearly write down what you intend to do or give in exchange for your desire and begin giving that now.

There is no such thing as something for nothing. The Law of Attraction is not about sitting around doing nothing and expecting to receive a big check in the mail for no reason at all. Generally, there is an exchange of energy. Now, that does not necessarily mean you will receive your desire from the exact same source as you are spending your energy.

For example, you may want to attract love. What can you give in exchange for that? What if you were to start being more loving to yourself, your friends, your family?

And if you want to attract more clients, what can you give in exchange for that? Perhaps you can start sharing your wisdom and insights through social media or live events.

Be careful here not to become attached to receiving in exchange for giving. Give unconditionally and purely. Do it for the enjoyment of doing it. You want to feel good while you are giving, not just doing it so that you receive.

Step 3: Gratitude Statements: Make your intention statement even more powerful by recognizing what you are already grateful for. Read Section 5, Technique #6 Gratitude, and create 10 Gratitude Statements which are relevant to your Desire and Intention statement. As you focus on gratitude, you feel good, which helps you raise your vibration in this specific area.

Emma's Statement:

Step 1. Desire (what I want to receive)

I am easily and efficiently attracting an abundance of new clients while making more time for myself.

Step 2: Intention (what I will give)

I consistently give great valuable content via social media channels

Step 3: Gratitude (what am I grateful for)

(Read: Section 5: Technique #6: Gratitude)

I am grateful for my business

I am grateful for my clients

I am grateful for my talents

I am grateful for my beautiful work environment

I am grateful for my health

Sam's Statement:

Step 1. Desire (what I want to receive)

I am ready and willing now to find an interesting person, who's just right for me and that I feel a strong connection with.

Step 2: Intention (what I will give)

I give love to myself and others by treating myself to at least one date per week, doing something fun and adventurous, either with myself r someone else.

Step 3: Gratitude (what am I grateful for)

(Read: Section 5: Technique #6: Gratitude)

I am grateful for my good looks

I am grateful for the time I have

I am grateful that someone is out there for me

I am grateful to have been loved

I am grateful for my job

Step 4: Keep this statement nearby (better yet, memorize it). Say it out loud 10 times throughout the day. Once when you first wake up. At least 8 times between waking and sleeping. Once again at bedtime.

Now it's your turn!

Exercise 5: Get Specific

Time: 20 minutes
Worksheet Available: Smart Goal
Download your worksheet at:
http://www.VictoriaMGallagher.com/ploabook

Let's get even more specific about your Desire Statement by turning it into a Smart Goal.

Read: Section 5, Technique #1 and create a S.M.A.R.T. Goal using your desire statement as the area of focus.

Condition #2 Thought

Defined: An idea or opinion produced by thinking or occurring suddenly in the mind.

> *"We are shaped by our thoughts; we become what we think. When the mind is pure, joy follows like a shadow that never leaves."*
>
> *- Buddha*

How do we get our thoughts in alignment with our desire?

Thoughts become things. It's where it all begins. Right? Or am I? Where do our thoughts come from? Is there something even before thought?

The conditions for manifesting are not linear.

Our results or manifestations are creating thoughts, beliefs, and feelings. As a matter of fact, the thoughts you have right now are most likely based on results you have already created at some point in your life.

If you're happy with the results you have in your life right now, then your thoughts and beliefs are likely positive and producing even more thoughts that make you happy. If you're disappointed by your results thus far, then your thoughts and beliefs are likely producing even more thoughts which cause you to feel more disappointment.

So, it could be argued that your past results give you your thoughts, yes?

Are you beginning to understand how this is not a linear process? We eventually must come into alignment with all the manifesting conditions at the same time.

Because of the sheer abundance of thoughts, you think daily, it's important to gain control of your thoughts and get them working for you, rather than against you.

The human brain produces somewhere between 50,000 – 70,000 thoughts per day. You can use them to train your brain for either success or failure.

Most of those thoughts are repetitive. About 95% of the thoughts you had today are the very same thoughts you had yesterday. Much of how you think is based off your belief system, which will be discussed in a bit.

You must change your thoughts to have the Law of Attraction work for you the way you want it to. If you're not sure how to go about this, take a pause and try this:

Exercise #1: Pause for 1 Minute

Stop everything you're doing right now and try not to think at all. Just stop reading and let yourself stop thinking for 1 minute. Ready? Set? Go!

(pause and stop reading for one minute)

Welcome back!

It's safe to assume you had at least 5 or 10 thoughts during the past 60 seconds that you were aware of. You never stop thinking. And as such, Law of Attraction never stops working.

Now, here's where it gets a little scary. Remember those 50,000 – 70,000 thoughts per day I mentioned, 95% of which are on auto-repeat? A whopping 70-80% of those thoughts are negative!

You might feel you are a positive thinker, but the problem is most of your thoughts are taking place at the subconscious level of your mind, below your conscious awareness.

If you ever wondered why you find yourself attracting negative things into your life, even though you say your affirmations and you think positive all the time, then it's time to look at the unconscious thoughts you most likely have.

You have subtle thoughts you're unaware of and noticeable thoughts that you are aware of. You don't usually notice your subtle thoughts. But they're there and they are likely impacting your results.

These thoughts are either about something you desire, or they are about something you fear.

I use the term fear to describe anything you are worried about or something you don't want.

It's your fear-based thoughts causing you to NOT manifest the results you DO want, and worse. These thoughts can manifest the exact opposite. Law of Attraction is not biased. It doesn't have a clue as to what you want. It doesn't work based on what you consciously say you want.

Your manifestations from Law of Attraction happen when you are in alignment with all conditions for manifesting. You could be in alignment with what you desire. Or you can be in alignment with what you fear.

If you have a fear you are going to fail in your business, whether it's conscious or unconscious, and that's what you are vibrating, then you are unknowingly creating at the level of infinite intelligence and it's sending you signals to act according to your fears!

So, you are literally going through all the conditions of manifesting, but in a way that attracts you toward the very thing you fear.

You must master your thinking. Your habitual thought patterns are automatic and completely impersonal. You can learn how to control your thoughts, so they are in alignment with your desires.

How to Master Your Thoughts

Discipline is necessary to master your thoughts. I am not suggesting you could possibly monitor every thought you have, or that all your thoughts are going to be positive. It isn't necessary to do that.

The subconscious is there for a reason. It's literally impossible to examine all 50,000 – 70,000 thoughts you have every day, even if you chose to spend the day doing nothing else.

It's the subconscious mind's job to help you sort and filter the millions of bits of data coming at you through your 5 senses.

In a way, you can think of it like a good spam filter. Only, your spam folder is filled with about 49,900 emails, and only 100 emails are coming into your inbox.

You naturally filter data based on how you've programmed it over the years to filter things. This is based on both your preferences and experiences.

And you know how sometimes, you get that pesky email that is junk, but it keeps going into your inbox until you deal with it?

Then, there are those emails you would find beneficial that are hiding in your spam folder. Those are likened to the missed opportunities available to you, which are all around you. They are not always visible because your brain is busy filtering data on automatic pilot so it's not showing you the ideas and opportunities that could help you make your dreams come true. It's showing you those ideas and opportunities that match the filters you set up in your belief system.

You are a change-resistant being. Change is stressful, and the subconscious mind tries to protect you from feeling stress because stress in the brain literally means you could die. So, it's not going to let you do that and it does a great job of keeping you safe.

How then, do you go about mastering your thoughts and getting them more in alignment with your desires?

Focus on what you Desire.

> *"Follow one course until successful."*
>
> *- Robert T. Kiyosaki*

Focusing the mind is one of the most crucial elements when it comes to Law of Attraction. It's also the most challenging.

One of the main causes of attracting what you don't want is focusing on what you don't want. You need to focus on what you do want.

You must know what you do want in order to focus on it.

In the **Desire** chapter, you created a desire and intention statement. You were asked to repeat your statement 10 times per day and that is one way to focus on it.

I often ask my clients, *"What do you want?"* They usually reply back with, *"Well, I don't want... And I don't want..."* When I say, *"So, tell me what you DO want,"* they will continue with the pattern of telling me what they don't want, until finally they come to an aha moment. *"Oh! I get it. I'm focusing on what I don't want."*

This pattern is ingrained in almost everybody's communication. It's how we talk. It's how we've learned to talk. It's not natural, but it's how we've learned to communicate. We hear the way other people talk about what they don't want, and it unconsciously becomes a pattern we pick up on.

For example, when I say, *"Don't think about a pink elephant,"* what are you thinking about? You're thinking about a pink elephant. But if I tell you, *"Okay, now I want you to think about a blue elephant,"* it's the same. You're going to be thinking about a blue elephant.

You need to get in the habit of catching yourself when you say what you don't want. Start to focus your attention and energy on what you do want instead.

Bottom line is this:

You get what you focus on.

In other words, focus on one thing at a time.

It is easy to get distracted. There are so many things you want right now. However, if you allow yourself to dart all over the place, trying to focus on too many goals at a time, then you are diluting your manifesting power.

If you were to focus on one idea only and allow other ones that come to your mind to pass, you have a far greater chance of success in that one thing. Then you can move on to the next thing.

Let's look at Soulmate Seeking Sam for example.

Sam hits the jackpot on Tinder one week, he's now dating 5 women. Spending Mondays with Susie and Tuesdays with Sally. He's going to miss some important details in those relationships and will not be able to get very deep in either one. Soulmate Seeking Sam needs to decide and choose one relationship to focus on and develop at a time, until he succeeds at finding his soulmate.

Follow

One

Course

Until

Success

In the case of Emma, the Entrepreneur, Emma wants to grow her life coaching business.

Emma needs a marketing strategy to grow her business and there are many choices that will work because there are a number of ways she can market her business. But, if she divides her attention between 10 different marketing strategies, she dilutes the power that would be available by focusing on a single strategy at a time.

We need to focus on one thing at a time.

How do you better develop your focus and not allow yourself to get distracted by all the shiny balls that are being thrown at you?

One of the best ways is through meditation.

Meditation is a great way to sharpen your focus, because it helps you develop your powers of concentration. A focused meditation, such as focusing on a specific object, is a great way to develop these skills. Meditation helps you increase your mental clarity. When you can take a few minutes out of your day to find that quiet space in your mind, you gather your energy and refocus your thoughts.

Let's do a simple meditation now!

Exercise #2: Meditation to Focus Your Mind

Time: 5 to 20+ minutes meditation, 5 minutes journaling
Worksheet Available: Meditation Reflections
Download your worksheet at:
http://www.VictoriaMGallagher.com/ploabook

Introduction to Meditation

Begin by setting a timer and choose to sit for a minimum of 5 minutes with your back straight.

Take a couple of deep breaths and notice the way the breath feels as it moves in and out of your mouth.

You can notice it by paying attention to your nostril area, your chest area, and then your belly.

As you focus on your breathing, you will notice the thoughts.

When you notice the thoughts, let them go and return your focus to the breath.

That is the essence of meditation.

By letting each thought go, it's helping you in your daily life by showing you how to let distractions and anything else go when they do not serve your highest good.

When you notice you have become attached to the thoughts, and you will, gently and calmly keep coming back to your breath.

Remember, you are just noticing the breath and not trying to breathe in any particular way.

The purpose of this exercise is to get control of your mind. If you can't control your thinking, how can you be in control of your life? Especially knowing what you think has a major influence over everything that happens in your life.

Simply witness your thoughts and learn to bring your focus back to your breathing. You will do this over and over, training yourself to focus and not be controlled by distractions.

Thoughts will come and go. You just don't need to engage with them.

Every day increase this for one minute. Ideally, meditate two times a day, morning and evening. Work your way up to 20 minutes per session.

Do it consistently at the same time every day.

Record your experience in the provided meditation reflections worksheet.

Condition #3 *Imagination*

Defined: The formation of a mental image of something. Form a mental image of; imagine.

> *"Imagination is everything. It is the preview of life's coming attractions."*
>
> *- Albert Einstein*

Another one of my favorite quotes by Albert Einstein is, *"Imagination is more important than knowledge. For knowledge is limited, whereas imagination embraces the entire world, stimulating progress, giving birth to evolution."*

The imagination is the most marvelous, miraculous, inconceivably powerful force the world has ever known.

Take a moment to think about this. Everything you see around you was once created in someone's imagination. It was in the imagination of Christopher Columbus that there was a New World, which caused him to set sail and discover what we now know as America. It was in the imagination of Benjamin Franklin, who invented the lightning rod conductor, which led to the exploration of electricity. If it was not for imagination, we would not have airplanes, automobiles, telephones, cell phones, computers, television, or radio.

All these ideas came from the imagination of ordinary men and women, just like you and me. We all have access to this creative power. It exists within us all.

And yet, the average person misuses their imagination in harmful and destructive ways.

In this chapter, I'm going to help you use your imagination the way it was intended to be used. To help you get into vibrational alignment between your desires, thoughts, and inner beliefs.

I use the words imagination and visualization interchangeably. They have similar meanings, but for the purpose of this chapter, when I say visualization, I want you to think of it as more of a tool, a technique, or a skill, a deliberate way of accessing your imagination.

When I say imagination, I am referring to the place, the faculty, where new ideas, images, and concepts are created and formed in one's mind.

Your imagination is a two-way communication system. Sometimes you are directly sending information to your imagination, generally through the process of visualization. However, your imagination is also capable of receiving information, as well. This tends to come in the form of intuition and inspiration. We'll be getting into how this works in later chapters, Creative Attraction and Inspired Action.

In chapter one, you set your desire and intention. In chapter two, you learned how to focus your thoughts. You discovered your thoughts need to be focused and in alignment with your desire.

When it comes to your imagination, it's extremely important to make sure that what you are imagining is also in alignment with your desire and your thoughts.

If you are suffering from self-doubt about how you will manifest your desire, your imagination is one of the best ways to develop faith and belief that your desire will manifest. It will also help encourage new beliefs within your subconscious mind.

To access the imagination, you will use the tool of visualization.

What is Visualization?

Visualization is a technique for forming mental images in your mind. It is one way to communicate your idea to your subconscious mind.

Visualizing is an important part of manifesting any desire. Visualization opens the doorway between the conscious mind and the subconscious mind. It allows you to speak directly to your subconscious mind and give it direct commands.

Remembering how the subconscious mind, unlike the conscious mind, has no ability to rationalize, it accepts the information you suggest without question.

Neurologists Know Visualization Creates a Better Future

Scientists working at the Wellcome Trust Centre for Neuroimaging at the Institute of Neurology in London have discovered people who visualize a better future are more likely to bring that future into existence.

Brain researchers have determined your subconscious doesn't know the difference between what is real and what is imagined. Therefore, every image you give the subconscious is believed to be real.

A classic example of this is to close your eyes right now. Imagine a lemon. A bright beautiful, yellow lemon. Using your vivid imagination, imagine yourself cutting the lemon in half. Bring the lemon up to your nose and smell its scent. Now, bring it up to your mouth and imagine biting into it. Taste the lemon in your mouth, feeling all the juices and the sourness.

When you open your eyes, notice what is happening in your mouth. If you have even the minutest imagination, you are very likely salivating right now.

The same thing happens whenever you watch a movie. You cry at the sad parts, and gasp and flinch at the scary parts. And that is because your subconscious mind experiences whatever you perceive and imagine as real and your body responds accordingly.

Suffice it to say that the language of your subconscious mind is images and feelings. You influence your subconscious mind through the faculty of your imagination. To give directions to your subconscious mind, it is best done using visualization.

Many people use visualization to inspire and motivate themselves. More than just thinking about your desire, visualization is the most effective tool to harness the power of your subconscious mind to help you manifest your desire.

Your subconscious mind has no choice but to bring you the desires you impress upon it, through your visualizations. Visualization is truly the key to creating the reality you desire.

The Skill of Visualization

Visualization is one of the most important skills a Law of Attraction student can gain mastery in. As with any other skill, such as speaking, communication, listening, creativity, relaxing, thinking positive, etc., some people are more naturally gifted at it than others. Those who already are visual have a natural knack for clearly communicating with their subconscious mind. If you are not a natural, it's perfectly fine.

Visualization is a skill anyone can develop and master. If you want to be successful at manifesting your desires, you must learn to visualize. Visualization serves as a valuable resource, not only in the area of achieving success, but in almost every area of your life.

Practicing your visualization skills will only require 5-10 minutes each day, and the results will be well worth the effort.

Before **you begin the visualization process**, let's go over some **helpful information** to dramatically improve your results.

Understand that everyone can visualize in some sense.

Occasionally, I find people who are concerned they aren't visual or that they can't visualize.

There are rare instances where a person cannot form any images in their minds. However, what people think of as visualization is seeing crystal clear, steady streaming, realistic images appearing in 3D. The ability to create images like that is also quite rare.

Often, visualization beginners start by seeing only very faint and fleeting images. They may rely more on other senses, perhaps they are more auditory or kinesthetic in nature. And it's perfectly fine to rely on your other senses if this happens to be the case with you.

If you are like most people, those who can bring images to your mind, but just not that well yet, practice this skill and you will get better at it.

The Visualization Technique

Exercise #1: Recall an Object

Wherever you are right now, look around and find something to focus on. It could be your hand, a painting, a glass of water, anything at all.

Stare at the object for about 15 seconds. Observe every detail as much as possible.

Then, close your eyes for about 30 – 60 seconds, take a deep breath, relax your mind. Recall the object in as much detail as possible. You will find that the more you allow yourself to relax and not strain to bring up the image, the easier you will be able to see the image in your mind.

Exercise #2: Envision Your Desire

Bring your desire to mind. Envision yourself now, having already accomplished your objective. To make it real, visualize all aspects of your life with this new reality. What other changes would result from achieving your desire?

For example, if you only imagine a big pile of cash on your dining room table, or money falling on you from the sky, that isn't suggesting to your subconscious mind you have achieved the amount of abundance you want. Does money really drop out of the sky? If you did have that much money, would you have it piled up on your dining room table? Probably not.

A more realistic image is a bank statement or brokerage statement showing the large bank balance. You might also see the individual payments that you get from your customers or from whatever source that money might be coming to you.

Also, consider anything else that would change in your life. Would you still be going to work every day? Would you be working in the same place? Would you be living in the same house? Drive the same car? Hang out with the same people?

Tip #1: Use whatever feelings and emotions come to you

While visualizing, you're likely to feel certain emotions. These emotions are the key to impressing your ultimate success onto your subconscious mind. If you feel confident and excited during your visualization process, it becomes more believable and more readily accepted by your subconscious mind.

We have many of our desires because we hope that by their attainment, they are going to make us feel something we don't currently feel. Happy, complete, loved, successful, confident, etc. But it works in reverse. To achieve our desires, we need to put ourselves into those states first, so that we become a vibrational match. It doesn't usually work the other way around.

Tip #2: Visualize frequently and consistently

You can't expect much if you only practice once a week. A good rule to follow is two times a day, minimum. The best times are while you're in bed: first thing in the morning and just before you fall asleep. Your mind tends to be more open and relaxed at these times.

Tip #3 Create a written visualization script and record yourself

Avoid trying to do it all in your head. Before beginning to visualize, begin with a written version. Write out your visualization and be as detailed as possible. What are your thoughts? How do you feel? What do you see, hear, taste, and smell? If you don't want to record yourself, you can read your visualization out loud twice a day. The more often and consistently you do this the better. The more senses and learning modalities you use, the better.

Tip #4: Imagine your dreams coming to life

Read your visualization out loud as if it is a story. This is much more effective than just occasionally daydreaming about your goals.

Emma's Visualization

While Emma might be very clear on her goals of success in her business, perhaps she spends too much time imagining things like clients cancelling. Or, she might look at her bank account dwindling. Seeing it go straight down to zero and having to file for bankruptcy is a thought she sometimes dwells on.

What she is imagining is not in alignment with her desire for a successful business.

Starting with Emma's **Desire and Intention Statement**, she now needs to make it come to life using the power of visualization. She would create a visualization script that describes the outcome of her desire. Seeing an abundance of clients, seeing the bank balance going up, enjoying the freedom of doing things that would require a larger bank account, such as travelling, living in a larger home, or doing other expensive activities that are in alignment with her desire.

Sam's Visualization

Sam has been looking for the love of his life and dating women using popular dating sites. He's created his desire statement, yet since he's been single for so long, he has a hard time imagining that he ever will meet that woman. He's used phrases like; *"all the good ones are taken"* and *"I'm happier just being single."* This is sending mixed signals to the universe.

While it can be frustrating when you're not meeting the right person, you still need to continue to send the universe clear messages about what you desire.

Going back to Sam's **Desire and Intention Statement**, he would create a visualization script that describes meeting and spending time with his soulmate. He might create a fantasy about how they ran into each other and met for the first time. Then, in future visualization sessions, continue the relationship in the way it would normally progress, and imagine every day scenarios that would take place as a relationship starts to form, such as having dinner together, sitting on the couch together, watching movies, travelling, meeting the family, etc.

Exercise #3: Create a Written Visualization Script

Time: 20 minutes
Worksheet Available: Visualization Script
Download your worksheet at:
http://www.VictoriaMGallagher.com/ploabook

Write a short, focused visualization script on your desire, according to the instructions above. One or two pages is just fine.

Exercise #4: Record Yourself Reading the Script.

Simply use any recording device you have available, your phone, your computer, and record yourself reading your script.

Exercise #5: The Visualization Process

Step 1: Make sure you're in a quiet environment without distractions.

Step 2: Begin by reading, listening to, or remembering your **Desire and Intention Statement** you created in Exercise 3 in the Desire chapter. Repeat the statement several times in your mind.

Step 3: Practice the Focus Your Mind Meditation for about 5 minutes.

Step 4: Play Your Recording.

Tips for Success:

- Visualize, using all 5 senses, on your desire. Focus on the details. Notice the colors, textures, sounds, and smells within your vision. See yourself touching the things in your vision and tasting the air.
- Let it play like a movie in your mind, with you as the director and leading star.
- Picture yourself already doing or having the things you want to manifest.
- See yourself accomplishing your goals with ease.
- Practice visualizing the thing you want at least two times each day. For visualization to work to its highest potential, you must be consistent with your new habit and use the practice every day.
- If you start to experience negative thoughts during your day, stop them and replace them with your vision and the positive thoughts connected to it.

Condition #4 Belief/Expectancy

Defined: Accept as true; feel sure of the truth of.

> *"Believe in yourself! Have faith in your abilities! Without a humble but reasonable confidence in your own powers you cannot be successful or happy."*
>
> - Norman Vincent Peale

I hesitate to suggest there is one manifesting condition that is more important than all the others, because without being in alignment with each of these manifesting conditions, you are not going to manifest your desire.

However, if I had to emphasize one manifesting condition, it would be belief.

Whatever you believe, is ultimately going to become your reality.

In order to manifest your desire, you must believe it will manifest!

There is a big difference between desiring something, thinking about it, visualizing it coming to fruition, and having the belief that it's going to happen.

One of the biggest reasons people fail to get what they want and throw in the towel on Law of Attraction is they fail to believe in their heart and with conviction, in their desire.

You may think you believe in your desire manifesting because you believe at a conscious level. You say, *"I believe!"* You write your affirmations. You picture it in your mind's eye. You draw pictures of it. Yet, the belief you have is superficial. Belief only at the conscious level of mind is not enough power to manifest your desire.

The visualization exercises are a great start to creating belief.

This is also where the levels of mind are important to understand.

Earlier I described the conscious mind, the subconscious mind, and the superconscious mind.

Until your beliefs have firmly planted themselves into your subconscious mind, you're going to continue manifesting whatever you currently believe is true at the subconscious level of mind.

Sometimes, blocks remain. I refer to these blocks as subconscious limiting beliefs.

What is a Limiting Belief?

For our purposes, here's our definition:

A limiting belief is one that is inaccurate and causes you to not live up to your highest or full potential.

Subconscious limiting beliefs are the story you have told yourself, or the story of your life or your past, which has been ingrained into your subconscious mind by your parents, by the people who raised you, by the people who influenced you, by past experiences, or by society in general.

Every belief in your subconscious serves you in some way. Your subconscious beliefs are there to protect you. They serve you. They keep you safe. They effectively block out any reality not in harmony with your current beliefs.

This can be a good thing, which is great. However, it can also be bad and when it is, challenges in implementing new improvements in your life occur.

Limiting beliefs stop you from reaching your highest potential. And they are the reason why you are not able to manifest certain things in your life. Or why you're not yet living the life of your dreams.

You need to learn how to discover and challenge your limiting beliefs.

The good news about the beliefs which reside in your subconscious mind is this. Once you create and install new empowering beliefs that align with your desire into your subconscious, they will begin to work for you, rather than against you. Now you are getting some help attracting your desire.

How Limiting Beliefs Affect Your Life

Limiting beliefs have a profound effect on our lives.

For example, you may have learned that people who make a lot of money are greedy, selfish, or bad in some way. You may have heard that from someone you respected and assumed it as your own belief, at an unconscious level.

At some point, you realize the belief is not true. However, it's still buried somewhere in your subconscious and it's guiding every decision you make and every action you take or don't take. That belief dictates how much money you'll allow yourself to earn.

Even though you don't believe that silly idea at a conscious level anymore, no matter what you do, you don't seem to be able to earn more than X amount of dollars.

You cannot force yourself to do something you inherently believe would make you a bad, selfish, or greedy person (like those filthy rich people).

So, if you ever want to break through your existing money set point, you'll have to change the beliefs you have about money at the subconscious level of mind.

Where do Limiting Beliefs Come From?

Limiting beliefs come from a variety of sources. Some of these sources might surprise you. Many of these sources were trying to help you, so don't cast blame on them. These people simply believed the wrong things.

Here are a few:

- **Family**. Most of our family means well, but many of our limiting beliefs come from familial sources and our suggestibility to comments from our families can vary. Maybe your mom told you that you couldn't run track in high school because you're too heavy, so now you believe that you could never be a runner.

Maybe your dad said that no one in his family ever went to college, so you believe it's not a possibility for you. Maybe you grew up in a lifestyle that was economically challenged so you decided that being wealthy was impossible for you.

- **Friends**. Much like our families, friends can do and say things that lead us to believe we're less capable than we are. Keep in mind that many of our friends don't want to see others do a lot better than they are doing. Also, other people tend to unintentionally push their limiting beliefs on others.

- **Teachers**. Teachers can have a lot of influence over us. When we're younger, they're almost like parents. Just like all people, teachers may make suggestions based on their own limiting beliefs and, in turn, they can easily be passed along on to their students.

- **Our own interpretation of events**. In many ways, this is probably the only real source of our limiting beliefs. For instance, it's not what your parents said to you, it's your interpretation of what was said to you.

For example, if your parents said, *"You'll never be able to get into college,"* you could believe what they've said is true or you could believe, *"They don't know what they're talking about. I can do it if I want."*

You can easily acquire limiting beliefs from any one at any time. Spouses, siblings, co-workers, what you read online, the news, and even the movies. All these sources can influence our thinking and create false beliefs and doubts about what is possible for us.

Exercise #1: Identify Your Limiting Beliefs

Time: 30 minutes
Worksheet Available: Limiting Beliefs
Download your worksheet at:<http://www.VictoriaMGallagher.com/ploabook>

To change anything, you must first identify it. Focus on eliminating one limiting belief at a time.

Step 1: Begin by choosing an area of your life that would have the most dramatic positive impact on your desire in life.

Step 2: Meditate for 5-10 minutes: Set a timer for 5 or 10 minutes (or even longer). Keep your pen and paper close by.

Close your eyes and take a few deep breaths to relax your mind.

Ask, *"What is limiting me from achieving my desire?"*

Listen to whatever is coming to you.

Continue asking the question any time your mind goes blank.

When the timer stops, thank your subconscious mind for helping you. Open your eyes. Spend a few minutes in silence, writing down everything that came to you during your meditation.

Step 3: Make a list of all your limiting beliefs.

Here's an example in the area of money:

- Making over $100k a year is hard.
- I'll never be wealthy.
- Rich people are dishonest.
- I'll never have enough money to have a nice house.
- If I'm rich, people will try to steal from me.
- My friends will treat me differently if I have a lot of money.

Can you see why it might be difficult to make a lot of money if you believe these things? Would you even be inspired to?

Exercise #2: Challenge Your Limiting Beliefs

Time: 20 minutes
Worksheet: Limiting Beliefs

Now, you have a list of your limiting beliefs around this area.

Consider whether the source of your belief is valid.

For example, did your limiting belief about money come from your mom? Was your mom a wealthy person? If she wasn't, then she's not a reliable source of information on that topic.

There is no such thing as a right or wrong belief. While a particular belief may be suitable for one person, it's totally disempowering for someone else to have that belief. It's a matter of whether having that belief is empowering or disempowering in relation to being in alignment with your desire.

Examine each of the limiting beliefs you have written down, one at a time.

Read the belief aloud and ask yourself:

- Is this belief accurate?
- Have I always believed this?
- Why do I believe this?
- Was there a time when I didn't believe this?
- Are there times when this belief doesn't make sense?
- Is there any evidence that disproves this limiting belief?
- What's the exact opposite way of thinking about this belief?
- What's funny about this belief?
- Is this belief helping me get what I want?

A funny example of finding out your belief is not true is when you hear a song and start singing along to it. You're convinced the words to the song go *"Wont you take me to my guitar..."* You've been singing it like this for years. Your friend hears you singing it one day. They stop you and say, *"Those are not the words, it's won't you take me to funky town!"* You're like, really? Uncertain at first, you play it back a few times. You hear the words correctly for the very first time. You're a bit stunned and a little embarrassed. You have a good laugh at yourself. Though it's even awkward at first, you start singing the right words from now on. You wonder, *"how did I not realize all these years I was singing it the wrong way?"*

Exercise #3: Create a New Empowering Belief

Time: 10 minutes
Worksheet: Limiting Beliefs

Rewrite a new belief that serves you. This will be the opposite of the limiting belief.

Your new belief needs to be believable to you. In other words, if you come up with a new belief you think is impossible and you have doubt it will happen, then it's most likely not going to manifest for you right now. For example. If you're limiting belief is *"it's hard to make $100k a year,"* don't suddenly try suggesting it's easy when you've always had a belief that it's hard. You could suggest something more believable like *"making $100k a year is possible for me."*

Exercise #4: Create Affirmations to Support this New Belief

Time: 20 minutes
Worksheet: Create Affirmations to Support the New Belief

Using the **Create Your Own Powerful Affirmations Technique** in Section 5, create a list of new affirmations to support your new empowering belief.

Here's what happens as Emma the Entrepreneur goes through the limiting beliefs exercises:

Step 1: She Begins by choosing money as an area of focus.

Step 2: She Meditates on her list for 10 minutes

Asking herself: *"What is limiting me from achieving success in business?"*

She comes up with:

"I'm not important enough to make 6 figures."

Step 3: She makes a list of her beliefs about money such as:

"I have to work hard for my money"

"I never have extra money"

"I don't deserve to make a lot of money"

Step 4: She begins with one of the beliefs she has written down and asks the challenge questions, *"Is this accurate?"* etc.

Step 5: She re-writes: *"I am important enough."*

"I now choose to value my worth and my time."

Step 6: She creates new affirmations that support this new belief.

"The work I do is important and much needed."

"I'm committed to valuing my time."

"Making 6-Figures is common for someone with my level of expertise."

Soulmate Seeking Sam discovers his limiting beliefs

Step 1: He begins by choosing finding love as an area of focus.

Step 2: He meditates on his list for 10 minutes

Asking himself *"What is limiting me from finding my soulmate?"*

He comes up with:

"There must be something wrong with me."

Step 3: He makes a list of his beliefs about finding love such as:

"There are no good people out there."

"No one will ever love me that much."

"I'm afraid I'll just get my heart broken again."

Step 4: He begins with one of the beliefs he has written down and asks the challenge questions, *"Is this accurate?"* etc.

Step 5: He re-writes: *"Finding the love of my life is worth putting myself out there again."*

Step 6: He creates new affirmations that support this new belief.

"I know the right person is out there looking for me."

"I'm willing to do whatever it takes to find love."

"Love is important and everyone deserves love, including me."

Exercise #5: Plant the New Belief in Self-Hypnosis

Time: 30 minutes
Worksheet Available: 3-10 Self Hypnosis
Download your worksheet at:
http://www.VictoriaMGallagher.com/ploabook

Read Section 5: Technique #3 Self-Hypnosis

Plant your new beliefs into your subconscious/

Condition #5 Feeling/Vibration

Defined: An emotional state or reaction.

> *"Everything is energy. Match the frequency of the reality you want, and you cannot help but get that reality. It can be no other way. This is not philosophy. This is physics."*
>
> - Albert Einstein

Most people say, *"I'll be happy when…"*

But it works the other way around.

You need to be happy first.

When it comes to manifesting, if you consider the theory that like energy attracts like energy, it means we attract to ourselves the energy that is in alignment with ourselves.

It's easy to get caught up in all our hopes, wants, and desires; to think having those things will fill some empty hole in us and make us feel a certain way.

After all, aren't those things supposed to make us feel good?

There are plenty of rich and successful people in the world who are unhappy. There are also people that have nothing, who are perfectly happy.

Things don't make us happy.

Being happy will align your vibration with the things you desire.

Not the other way around. You attract according to how you are being.

Getting what you want only provides temporary satisfaction.

To attract what you want, you must begin at the end; how you want to feel.

Ask yourself: What do you want? Then ask why you want that? Keep asking why until you get down to the feeling or state you want. Security, peace, fulfillment, happiness, love, etc.

Having identified the feeling you want, find simple ways to feel that way.

How do you cause yourself to feel happy?

First, understand it's not entirely your fault that you don't always feel happy.

Our brains are predisposed to paying more attention to negative things than positive.

It's a habit we have learned from our early ancestors who had to defend themselves against threats—like being eaten alive by saber-tooth tigers. Though these threats no longer exist, our brains are still wired with those survival instincts, which keep us on high alert for the bad stuff that could be right around the next corner.

If you are expecting a positive result, you are going to feel positive. If you expect a negative result, you are going to feel negative.

When it comes to Law of Attraction, our feelings guide us to know whether we are on the right track toward manifesting what we want.

If you are too obsessed with the desire, you might feel the lack of it, rather than the abundance of it.

For example, you want to manifest a big house.

The positive way to focus on it is every time you look at that house, you get extremely excited by it. You don't care how it's going to happen. It doesn't even matter when it's happening. You just know you're moving into that house. You feel peaceful, patient, and thrilled. That's how you truly feel when you know something is happening. You're playful about it. You mentally prepare yourself. You imagine the furniture you'll be buying. You see yourself driving home to that house, cooking, entertaining, and all the usual things you'll do once you move in.

That makes you feel good.

The negative way to focus on it is to look at your existing place where you live. You look at the small spaces, the out of date blinds, the old carpet, and you go, *"boy, I'll sure be glad when I get my new house and I don't have to deal with this stupid place anymore!"*

You look at the house you want. You sigh, and say, *"How much longer is it going to take before I can move out of this dump?"* You're so focused on how annoying this place is where you now live. You see someone else living in a great place, like the one you want, and you think, *"Some people have all the luck!"*

That makes you feel bad.

Rather than focusing on what you don't want, work toward getting yourself into alignment with the feeling state of being in that big house right now.

Are you taking care of the place you are in now with the same love and care as you would put into owning the big house? What is one glaring issue in your current place? Is there a way to make it better? Perhaps you are feeling the closets are too small. There are not enough drawers. Things need fixing up.

Rather than dwelling on things like, *'these closets are too small,'* go through your closet and get rid of some of the clutter. Donate some of those old clothes and shoes. Fix up some of the broken things. Show some respect to the place you are in, and yourself at the same time. Make your current situation as enjoyable as you can possibly make it. This is a great way to express your gratitude and appreciation for what you have now. You will surely raise your vibration, feel more present, and less desperate.

This same rationale holds true regardless of what you desire to manifest. A nicer car, a better job, your dream body, or a relationship. Make the most out of what you have now. That is going to put you into a much more inspired mindset while you are working toward manifesting your bigger desire.

What is Vibration?

You have been learning throughout the previous chapters, how to align your thoughts, imagination, beliefs, and feelings with what you desire, and these conditions all have an impact on your vibration.

If you're unfamiliar with the word vibration in the context I am referring to, let me explain a little more.

How do your thoughts, feelings, emotions, and vibration all work together?

First, our thoughts can trigger an emotion.

Emotions are unconscious, chemical responses felt in the body in response to *stimuli*. That stimuli could be any external or internal experience.

Feelings are at the conscious level of mind. They are how we mentally perceive our emotions. Everyone perceives emotions differently.

Emotions are energy. They are always in motion.

Throughout the day your emotions will vary in intensity and flow between extremely positive to extremely negative.

When we are not experiencing the highs and lows, we all tend to fall back on a predominant emotion.

That predominant fallback emotion is essentially your set point energy vibration.

Why do we care about our energy vibration?

Your energy vibration is the energy which everyone feels whenever they are around you.

You've experienced people who give off some sort of energy vibe that is either attractive or repulsive.

That is what I am talking about. That is vibration.

We live in a vibrating universe.

Everything is vibrating.

Everything is energy.

Your energetic vibration is what causes you to keep attracting things that match that energy vibration into your life.

When you actively work toward raising your vibration, you align yourself and your desire.

Everything discussed so far in this book is part of what goes into raising your vibration.

Knowing you attract things to you based on how you're vibrating, you have to become self-aware of your vibrations.

How you'll know whether you are sending a positive or negative vibration is by noticing how you're feeling.

There are basically two root emotions. Those which come from love and those which come from fear. Countless emotions exist in between.

Love-based emotions, such as gratitude, appreciation, joy, empowerment, passion, and happiness send a positive vibration. They make you feel good.

Fear-based emotions, such as hatred, anxiety, anger, frustration, disappointment, doubt, and depression send a negative vibration. They make you feel bad.

The more strongly you feel an emotion, the stronger the vibration you are sending, whether negative or positive.

If you are predominately hovering around a particular energy vibration, then you are going to be more of a match for people, experiences, and circumstances that are at the same vibration.

What can you do to raise your energy vibration?

You first need to become aware of what emotions you are feeling. Your feelings are your guide that tells you what vibration you are emitting.

Can you identify what you are feeling right now?

Would you say you are experiencing an emotion coming from love or from fear?

If the emotion is coming from love, great! You're sending a positive vibration. You know you're on the right track. Your trusting the process. You feel happy, excited, committed, inspired, and enthusiastic. There's no doubt. No attachment to the outcome, and you're moving full steam ahead, taking all the necessary actions.

If the emotion is coming from fear, you're sending negative vibrations. This is a sign something is out of alignment. You do not trust the process. You feel sad, depressed, doubtful, lazy, and stuck. You're putting off the actions you need to take. There's lots of doubt. You're attached to feeling the emotion because you're avoiding it.

To raise your energy vibration begins with awareness, acceptance, and letting go of resistance.

Let Go of Resistance

Do you try to push down your emotions? Do you attempt to pretend you're happy? Fake it till you make it? Or do you just try to forget about them?

In a way, it's a lie you're telling yourself.

Carl Jung contended that *"what you resist not only persists but will grow in size."*

Holding onto negative emotions and not dealing with them will keep you unconsciously attached to them.

You can ignore your emotions, but they're still there and they're still emitting a vibe.

Be Present

How you deal with your emotions is all about learning the art of accepting and embracing the emotion in the moment.

Welcome what is. The more you accept and knowledge the emotion, the more you will be able to let it go.

Take a few moments to just be with whatever emotion is there. You don't need to put words to it. It doesn't need to mean anything. There is no need to attach any stories to how you feel. Simply place your awareness on it and allow it the freedom to be expressed.

This goes for negative and positive emotions and feelings. As a matter of fact, if you are experiencing a mild positive emotion, just by witnessing that, you may find yourself able to move into an even better emotion. Just feel, accept, and allow.

I find meditation to be one of the best ways to not only get present but improve your ability to stay present for longer moments at a time.

For best results, spend a minimum of 20 minutes a day in meditation. Work your way up to 20 minutes in the morning and 20 minutes in the evening.

I've provided two meditation techniques in this book:

- **Meditation to Focus Your Mind** found in Section 3: Condition #2 Thought - Exercise #2.
- **Vipassana Meditation** found in Section 5: Techniques to Raise Your Vibration – Technique #4.

Detachment

Here's the tricky part about manifesting.

When you are experiencing negative emotions and feelings, it's most likely because you are attached to the result. Being attached to the results essentially means you don't think it's going to happen. When you are attached to something, you feel clingy, scared, paranoia, anxious, frustrated, and irritated.

If you have concrete deadlines for your goal to manifest, you might start to feel impatient, especially if the deadline approaches or even passes.

How to detach:

Take your focus off the results and place it on the actions in the here and now. Stay present. Enjoy the process.

Focusing only on results creates resistance.

If you spend every moment just getting through it, doing stuff you dread doing for one shining moment of achievement, you are going to spend most of your life feeling unhappy. You're going to miss out on the 99.9% of life that happens in between. If you have to do things in order to get to the end result that don't make you happy or fulfilled, then you are definitely not pursuing the right goal.

The real joy of life is found in the journey.

The key to detaching is to place all your attention on the present. Are you enjoying whatever you're doing right now? Let everything go and just enjoy the moment, feeling relaxed and happy. The more you appreciate this endeavor, guess what, the more you are turning up the feeling good state and raising your vibration.

It is no coincidence that taking your attention off the result and being happy now is exactly what is going to raise your vibration and speed up your manifestation.

Don't make what you do just a condition to get a result. Your actions should feel fulfilling and you should sense your passion about all you love doing.

For example, many people fall into a trap of figuring out an idea, so they can make a lot of money. Yet, they force themselves to do things they don't like. That is no approach to a great life. You must do things the other way around. Do the things you love doing and you will be taken care of financially. If you aren't loving it, then there is something else out there for you.

Stop limiting yourself with a demand for specifics on the exact way, how, or when it will happen. You cannot force the universe to give you what you want exactly the way you want it. It's a partnership, a collaboration. And you need to be willing to do your part and trust your partner (the universe) is doing theirs.

What if your desire doesn't manifest in the exact way you are hoping it will? Are you going to be ok? Or are you going to let that destroy you? What if there was something even better waiting for you? If only you would let go of the firm grip on your attachment to this idea.

Playing the *"What if"* scenario is a great way to gain peace of mind about your desire not manifesting, while still gently focusing on it.

To play the *"What if"* scenario, simply ask yourself, what if my desire didn't manifest? What if there is something better? Then make up a story about how it could play out even better.

For example:

Emma's been attached to growing her coaching practice to a 6-figure a year income.

She's made the same goal every year, yet still only making $50,000 a year.

What can she do to get detached?

She uses the *"What if"* scenario and asks, "*What if I don't grow my business to $100k this year?*"

She could look at being offered an amazing opportunity to travel and speak to high level executives for $75,000 a year, a lesser amount of money but it's guaranteed. This alternative future may feel even better since she's still making more money, she gets to travel, and still do coaching calls on the road.

Sam has been attached to finding his soulmate.

He's now been single for 3 years.

What can he do to get detached?

Sam asks, "*What if I don't find my soulmate this year?*"

He could create an alternative plan where it took two years to manifest, but it was due to some fortunate twists that took him out of the country where he ended up meeting the love of his life.

The High Vibe Makeover

As I mentioned, the joy of manifesting is in the journey. Are there actions you are taking to try and manifest your desires which you absolutely hate doing?

I do a weekly podcast, called **Power of Your Mind**. I love the interviewing and recording. However, I really don't like having to edit all my recordings or write the descriptions and post them anymore. Due to that, I was getting slowed down and preventing myself from booking more podcast interviews. I decided to stop doing the editing myself and get someone else to do it.

When you can take one thing off your plate that you don't like doing, then you have room to replace it with things you do like instead. So, instead of editing the recordings, I have replaced that time with doing more Facebook live interviews, which I enjoy a whole lot more. As it turns out, this raises my vibration. I feel good when I'm doing it. I gain exposure and experience. This gets me closer to my desire to do 100 paid public speaking gigs each year.

Emma dislikes dealing with tech stuff. It is mind-numbing to her. So, she chooses to outsource any technical projects that take more than 20 minutes.

Now that she has a bit more free-time, she chooses to spend more time out in nature, hiking, meditating and taking her mind off her business for a while.

Sam grew tired of the monotonous online dating cycle, where he felt obligated to take women out for expensive dinners and surface conversations, Sam came up with other creative, fun and inexpensive ideas for meeting up instead.

He created a task list of daily things he can do to increase his feelings of self-love, such as meditating, reading, taking himself out on dates, etc. and performs one task each day.

Exercise #1: The What if Scenario

Time: 10 minutes
Worksheet Available: What if Scenario
Download your worksheet at:http://www.VictoriaMGallagher.com/ploabook

Ask Yourself: What if my desire didn't manifest?

Discover new possibilities. Write a story about the desire you want not manifesting. Come up with an alternative situation and how it surprisingly ended up even better.

Exercise #2: High Vibe Makeover

Time: 20 minutes
Worksheet Available: High Vibe Makeover
Download your worksheet at:http://www.VictoriaMGallagher.com/ploabook

Step 1: Are you spending time doing activities which lower your vibration? List any daily activities you do which you do not like. Is there any way to achieve the desired result without having to spend time doing things you dislike?

Step 2: List any daily activities, related to your desire which you enjoy doing? Can you commit to retiring one undesirable activity with spending more time doing what you enjoy?

Condition #6 Creative Attraction

Defined: The action or power of drawing forth a response: an attractive quality.

> *"It is the combination of thought and love which forms*

the irresistible force of the law of attraction."

- Charles F. Haanel

You might have thought creativity is something only scientists, artists, musicians, or poets have. This is not the case—every one of us has immense untapped creativity.

Every child is born with extraordinary creativity.

In 1968, George Land conducted a research study to test the creativity of 1,600 children ranging in ages from three-to-five years old who were enrolled in a Head Start program. This was the same creativity test he devised for NASA to help select innovative engineers and scientists. The assessment worked so well he decided to try it on children. He re-tested the same children at 10 years of age, and again at 15 years of age. The results were astounding.

Test results amongst 5-year-olds: 98%

Test results amongst 10-year-olds: 30%

Test results amongst 15-year-olds: 12%

Same test given to 280,000 adults: 2%

Children are naturally imaginative and innovative. They're curious. Then, as they grow up, they become bombarded by authority figures who tell them their ideas are foolish or silly. They must color between the lines. Don't touch this, smell that, taste this, or get into that. Gradually children adapt to the instructions and learn at a deep subconscious level, it's wrong to go off the beaten track.

Fortunately, the creative faculty is never totally lost. It just becomes dormant. It can be awakened; you can begin to use your creativity again, whenever you choose.

Where Does Creativity Come From?

The source of pure creativity is a function of the superconscious mind, which we discussed earlier in The Superconscious Mind chapter.

All creative geniuses, innovations, and breakthroughs throughout history are sourced from the superconscious mind. The superconscious mind is collective, universal, and impersonal.

Here's how it works:

You've had the experience of struggling with some problem or trying to achieve a goal. Then, as you're walking or driving along, it just hits you. An idea bursts into your mind like a bolt of lightning. It's the perfect idea. That idea is coming from the superconscious mind.

I'm sure you've had the experience of thinking about someone and the phone rings and it's them. Or you call someone else and they say, *"I was just thinking about you."*

We've all had experiences when the superconscious mind has been working in our lives.

Two of the most common terms we use to explain experiences resulting from the superconscious mind are: serendipity and synchronicity.

Serendipity is the occurrence and development of events, which happen by chance, in a happy or beneficial way. Sometimes people write-off these experiences as coincidence.

Synchronicity is the simultaneous occurrence of events which appear significantly related but have no discernible connection.

Sometimes you receive these inexplicable waves of insight that come from **out of the blue.**

Where do these insights come from? Are you paying attention to them?

One of the greatest musicians of all time, **Mozart**, wrote his music note-perfect, without corrections or changes needed, the very first time. When he sat down to write, he said the entire symphony would come into his mind and he would simply transcribe it onto paper.

Beethoven, who was deaf from the age of 35, said the symphonies came full blown into his mind and he simply transcribed them on paper.

Many people can get parking spots 20 out of 20 times on crowded city streets. All you do is clearly visualize a parking stall in front of the building where you want to park.

How to Work with the Superconscious Mind

The superconscious mind works by sending and receiving information through your subconscious mind.

Imagine you had access to the mother computer which connects with the entire network of all computers in the universe. This is the most complex, sophisticated computer ever built. You have also amassed an entire team of the savviest computer geniuses. They are at your service 24 hours a day, 7 days a week. You could present them any problem or goal and they could hack into the entire network of intelligence and bring you the answer.

However, even with the most sophisticated computer system and the most intelligent computer operators there is absolutely nothing they can do for you if you do not clearly tell them what you desire.

That is why it is important to have a very clear specific idea of your pure desire. The clearer you are about what you desire, the more quickly the superconscious mind can get to work to bring the answers to you.

Therefore, it is extremely important for you to always keep your mind focused on what you want to happen.

Every person who becomes successful, sooner or later, developed the habit of meticulous focus on what they want to happen. Rather than on what they fear.

How to send messages to the superconscious:

You must talk about, think about, visualize, and imagine only that, which you desire to come into your reality.

Any thought, belief, desire, or vision held continuously in your conscious mind must be brought into reality by the superconscious mind.

How to receive information from the superconscious:

Let it go and act on your intuition to carry out the instructions given to you.

Getting back to our computer geniuses. They've received clear instructions from your subconscious mind. They immediately work out the solution to bring you the results you want. They inject into the imagination faculty of your brain all the ideas, intuition, insight, and instructions you need, to take the first step to carry out your desire.

This usually happens at a random time when you've completely detached from the request you made.

The most important thing you can do is act on the answer immediately when it comes to you. Don't hesitate in implementing the intuition, insight, idea, or answer which comes. This is essential.

When you begin working with the superconscious mind, it's like getting a muscle into shape.

The more you tap into it, the faster and better it works to your benefit. It will finally get to the point where you can think of a goal or put a problem into the superconscious mind and you'll get a response sometimes within minutes, sometimes so fast it will astound you.

Develop a sense of urgency and act instantly. When you receive those gems of insight from the superconscious mind, the more rapidly you act on those insights the more insights you'll receive.

Here's a fun and simple way to expand your creativity and connect with your intuition.

You are going to create a laboratory or whatever you want to call it, which is always there for to tap into all kinds of new ideas. You'll relax and quiet your mind first then set it up as follows:

Step 1: Create a work space environment in your mind and design it exactly however you would want it in a perfect world.

Somewhere that is peaceful and feels creative for YOU. This room can be big or small, light or dark, or anything you choose. It can be very sterile or like a magical castle. Whatever suits you. Perhaps it's a big office with lots of room, a studio, or an actual laboratory.

Step 2: Put yourself inside this space and add tools, objects, furnishings, and decoration. Anything that would help you enhance your imagination.

You might add things like a large screen, whiteboards, books, computers, a table and chairs. An examination table with magical potions. It could have multiple rooms. An elevator or a door where helpful people can enter. This is your laboratory, so feel free to include whatever you think would be helpful.

Step 3: Finally, you'll add a board of advisors, helpful people, or guides for assistance.

These are people that are on call and available to you whenever you need assistance. You can call these people into the room any time you want to receive advice or guidance. You may even imagine being able to communicate with people you admire who can motivate you or inspire you.

The more imaginative and childlike you are, the better this works.

Sam has created his laboratory in the style of a beautiful house, which has lots of decorations and furnishings and a feminine touch. He sits on his couch and invites into his laboratory a relationship expert and asks him for advice about finding his soulmate. After an enlightening conversation for about 5 minutes, he's received some insightful answers and he thanks the expert for his help. He immediately puts the advice into action.

Emma has a large, very modern looking healing sanctuary in the middle of a forest, which is decorated with inspirational wall art, words, and plants. She sits at a large desk with two of her advisors sitting across from her and they conduct a business strategy meeting. She interviews them on their top ten principles of successful entrepreneurship. This 20-minute meeting proves extremely insightful. She thanks them for their input and goes straight to work on implementing the strategies she received during this powerful session.

Now it's your turn:

Exercise #1: The Laboratory in Your Mind

Time: 20 minutes meditation, 5 minutes journaling
Worksheet Available: Laboratory Reflections
Download your worksheet at:
http://www.VictoriaMGallagher.com/ploabook

As often as possible, as little as weekly or as often as daily, spend anywhere from 10 - 20 minutes in your laboratory whenever you want to access your creative genius.

Record your experience in the provided laboratory reflections worksheet.

What ideas did you receive?

What actions can you take?

Condition #7 Inspired Action

Defined: The process of doing something, arising from creative impulse, to achieve something extraordinary.

> *"Everything you want is out
> there waiting for you to ask.
> Everything you want also wants
> you. But you have to take action
> to get it."*
>
> *-Jack Canfield*

What distinguishes a person who succeeds with Law of Attraction with one who fails to manifest what they want?

The willingness and speed with which they take inspired action.

No matter how much you wish, hope, desire, pray, dream, meditate, ask, believe, have faith, and everything else it takes to manifest, it ultimately comes down to the action you take.

It's necessary to set intentions and visualize your outcome. However, in order to succeed, you have to take action. Action is often the missing link in the law of attraction. Not just any action though.

You're not manifesting anything by sitting on your couch, meditating all day long, and waiting for something to bring your desire to you.

However, if you are meditating, visualizing, and intending your desire all day and consistently, you would be receiving inspiration. This would inspire and compel you to get up and go after it.

The point is, action on your part is a requirement.

This chapter and the Creative Attraction chapter work hand in hand. In Creative Attraction, I discussed how an idea comes to you from the imagination faculty in the form of an idea, intuition, or insight.

Now you're going to carry out the ideas and manifest your desire.

There're literally endless possibilities of how this could happen for you. The inspiring actions you need to take are those seemingly small thoughts, nudges, or hunches you may normally dismiss and are not in the habit of pursuing.

This call-to-action comes from a variety of places; in the form of a thought, a sign, a conversation with another person, hearing something in a movie, reading something, or a repeating pattern. Inspired action is the way that the superconscious guides you in the direction of your desire.

You must be very present in order to hear this call.

Let me clarify a few things about taking inspired action.

Inspired action feels like the right thing to do. If you were to look back from the future after your desire has manifested, you would see the path you took is full of twists and turns you never anticipated when you set out on your journey.

It's seldom a straight line to manifestation. Many times, we have obstacles in our way that we need to clear from our path in order to get where we are going. At times, it can look like your life is falling apart before everything falls into place.

You could never truly know every step along your path to manifesting your desires, before you take the first step. You have to take the first step, then follow the signs and signals which lead you toward your desire.

Inspired actions are not typically big, hairy, audacious steps. They are usually small steps which may lead to big changes over time.

For example, you are probably not going to get a message that it's time to start a new job or business, to get divorced, or make a drastic change in your health.

You'll receive messages with much smaller clues. For example, if it's about starting a new business, it's likely to be in an area you feel passionate about. You may notice other people telling you how knowledgeable you are in that area. They'll suggest *maybe you should start a business*. The suggestion may get confirmed by other signs. You may see ads for small business loans. A book about starting a new business may appear to you out of the blue. You will continually see patterns around starting your new business.

The more you sharpen your awareness and tune into your intuition, the more you will be able to recognize these signs as the universe communicating with you. Sometimes people confuse this with coincidence.

When you have every opportunity come knock on your door yet continue to ignore the signs and look for more information, you are not allowing the universe to work through you.

Sometimes we get in our own way by trying to figure it out. The signs you are getting might not make any logical or rational sense. This is what's funny about inspired action. It's going to feel different. It might feel strange. It's going to probably be a little uncomfortable.

Why? Because everything you know and have right now is something that rests within your present level of awareness.

If you do what you've always done, then you'll have what you've always had.

To get something you've never had before you must act in a manner that falls outside of your present level of awareness. These signs are there to help you expand your awareness and move beyond your comfort zone.

When these specific signs present themselves to you, you need to investigate them. Literally, if you are feeling inspired to take a new way home or turn here or there, be willing and prepared to act on it. Be spontaneous and just do it.

Inspired Actions versus Forced Actions

Forced actions are those in which you are trying to make something work. Imagine you have a square peg and you're trying anything you can to fit it into a round hole because that's what you feel needs to be done. It doesn't work well, does it?

Now imagine inspired action. With this, you are feeling compelled to do something. You may not even be certain why, but taking the step feels significant to you. You're excited about doing it, even when there is no logical reason why. For example, if you've been missing a deceased parent and you can't seem to shake it, you may have one of those sudden ideas pop into your thoughts suggesting you finally get to cleaning out that old box of things you've been delaying doing. You go down and do it, discovering something which serves as a warm reminder of your deceased parent. These are the moments when you realize that you were somehow guided toward just what you needed.

So, how do you know if an action is an inspired action?

Your hint lies in how you feel when you do the action.

There is no right or wrong actions to take.

One action can be great for one person and a bad idea for another person.

Forced Actions make you feel:	Inspired Actions make you feel:
Obligated	Fun
Unnatural	Easy
Imposed	Motivated
Strained	Time goes by fast
Pressed	Inspired
Stifled	Good
Struggle	Happy
Anxious	Enjoyable
Tired	Flow
Impatient	Natural
Fear	Excited
Hard work	
Time goes by slowly	Alive
Figuring out	True
Attachment	Gentle
Doubt	Unexpected
Procrastination	Allowing
Frustration	Energized

A common reaction for people in the forced action category is the compulsion to take more action. Try to fight procrastination. Push even harder. Work more. Do more.

The truth of the matter is, most people don't have a problem acting. Some people are addicted to taking action. People who have a strong desire are not lazy. The thing preventing most people who are not taking action from doing so is the lack of certainty about which actions to take. Compare this to others who just act, act, act. When one thing doesn't work, they research it, figure it out, and come up with a new plan. They'll just keep pushing, pressing, and struggling. This is not sustainable because that person will eventually crash and burn.

When you notice you're trying to force a goal, stop for a moment and think about it. Why is this a struggle for you? Why are you fighting what you claim to desire? Why are you sabotaging yourself? Why do you keep procrastinating?

You're going to want to spend your day feeling passion and joy for what you're doing. Why do it if you don't enjoy it? Think about it. You have a desire to have a successful business. You've defined that success as making a six- or seven-figure income. You work 12, maybe 15 hours a day, doing activities you don't enjoy doing. The day may never come when you can say you make the money you want to make. And so, you will have done all the work you don't like, toward a goal which never manifests for you.

Conversely, that day does arrive when you finally break through to that level of income. Are you happy now? No, because you must continue to do the work you don't like in order to sustain that income level. You may have felt a temporary moment of satisfaction, but you will never be happy working to try and make a certain amount of money.

Or let's say your goal is to be married one day. So, you go out on a lot of dates in order to try and find the one to get married to. But, when you go out on these dates, it feels like a grueling process. You feel like you are just going through the motions. You're not even present to the moment when you're out on a date. You're so focused on getting married you can't even hear what your date is saying. Whether or not this person is the right one for you, you are either thinking your date is wrong for you and you're not enjoying yourself, or you're thinking they are the person of your dreams. *When can we go ahead and get married?*

The key to inspired action is you need to enjoy the actions you are taking more often than not.

Let's be realistic. You are not going to enjoy every single moment of every single day while you are in pursuit of your desire. Whatever you are doing, even if the thing is not enjoyable, such as driving in heavy traffic or waiting in line, challenge yourself to enjoy even the most mundane, non-pleasurable actions. The more you enjoy the actions you take the more life guides you toward actions you'll enjoy.

To take inspired action, you need to create a new habit of listening to the guidance from within—your intuition. Trust your intuition. It's there to help you. And act, immediately on whatever it is telling you. The sooner you act, the sooner you will gain further insight into what you need to do next. That is how you are also getting your actions into alignment with your desire. The process of manifesting your desire should be enjoyable.

What you desire and every step in between that and the manifestation of it is in alignment, as are your actions. Each action leads to the next. It becomes an adventure which unfolds as you respond to the guidance you are receiving, bringing you closer to your desires in a way that feels…well, inspired!

What you need to get is this: It's not about the happiness in the end that you'll get when you manifest. The *feel good* is in the action.

The action, itself, feels good.

The act, itself, is energizing, exciting, and fulfilling.

You wake up ready and willing to act for the sheer joy of getting to take those actions.

If you are not sure if you are receiving any inspiration yet to take an action, then you can make that your intention each day. Before doing anything, meditate on being shown at least one inspired action.

And before long you will feel inspired every day toward which actions are best for you to take and you'll want to take them.

Giving is an Inspired Action

To be truly in alignment with the laws of nature, it's equally important to give as it is to receive.

Giving and receiving are two sides of the same coin. You cannot have one without the other. It's an energy flow which keeps the manifesting energy in constant circulation. When one of these energies is closed, it can block the flow of energy all together. Conversely, if you are always giving, but you have a hard time receiving, that can also block the flow.

Giving, just for the sake of it, makes you feel happy. To do something that spreads a little joy to someone else feels good and therefore, it raises your vibration.

Some people find themselves putting off giving until after their desire has manifested. Remember that everything is happening simultaneously. There is no need to wait for abundance to show up because the abundance is already there. You just have not yet observed it. The act of giving puts you in harmony with the abundant universe. It's an expression that states, I have plenty to give.

The essence of true giving is unconditional. Never make your giving conditional or expect to receive something in return. Often, when you give, the universe gives back, but it's not usually an exact exchange nor does it come from the same source. The more you can give without expecting anything, just for the joy of it, the more likely you are to receive pleasant little surprises at random times in your life.

Of course, always give responsibly and within your means. Being generous does not necessarily mean giving money or things. There are many ways to give. You can give your time, advice, listen, a smile, or you can give affection in the form of a hug. You can donate to your favorite charity or to someone else's. Offering a service or a favor is a wonderful way to give.

If your desire entails looking for a new career, for example, giving your very best effort in your present career is one great way to propel yourself into the right vibration to attract you in the direction of new opportunities. Similarly, if you are looking for love, give love. Love is attracted to love, so the more love you give, the more love you receive.

What are some examples you can think of that you can easily take on for the next 30 days to get into the giving habit?

Emma wrote in her intention statement that she will give great advice, tools, and techniques in the area of self-improvement.

One way that she could do that - even before she has clients - is she can create a blog where she offers helpful tools, tips and strategies to her target audience. She could also give away a free helpful eBook of tips and tricks to improve your life. By giving this, she attracts the attention of possible clients.

In Sam's intention statement, he wrote what he would give is love.

Sam would find ways to give love in an enjoyable way. This might mean practicing self-love, being more loving in his current relationships with his family and friends. As he increases that outward flow of loving energy, he is creating a magnetic vibration and radiating love. He might also choose to perform one random act of kindness toward himself and others every day.

Exercise #1: Inspired Action

Time: 10 minutes
Worksheet Available: Daily Action Journal

Download your worksheet at:
http://www.VictoriaMGallagher.com/ploabook

How do you take inspired action?

You can't conjure up inspired action, because those are the actions you're going to take immediately when you receive insights, ideas, hunches, that are sent to you from the superconscious mind so there is not a proactive approach that you can take this instant to take inspired action.

Continue to work with your laboratory exercise, from the *Creative Attraction* chapter. The more you do that exercise, the more you will strengthen your connection with the superconscious. You are bound to receive the ideas as to what step to take next. When you do, act immediately.

Exercise #2: Action by Giving

Time: 10 minutes
Worksheet Available: Intentional Giving Journal
Download your worksheet at:
http://www.VictoriaMGallagher.com/ploabook

Revisit your *Desire and Intention Statement* from the *Desire* chapter. In that exercise, you were asked to '*Clearly write down what you intend to do or give in exchange for your desire and begin giving that now.*'

Decide what and how you will give and begin giving it. Spend part of your day doing the activity you said you would give in exchange for your desire. This activity should make you feel good. The time it takes for this varies, depending on the activity, but as you increase the amount of giving, you are opening yourself up to receive.

Always be in the process of giving. The more you give, the more you put the energy out there, the more it does (eventually) come back to you.

Condition #8 Manifestation

Defined: To make evident or certain by showing or displaying.

> *"The outcome that we wish suddenly manifests itself in our reality, and the truth is, none of those things suddenly appeared. It is we who have suddenly appeared on the scene where they existed always."*
>
> - Neale Donald Walsch

Having studied and applied the conditions in each of the previous chapters, you should be more in alignment with, and well on your way toward, the manifestation of your desire.

This would not be the first time you've ever manifested—just maybe deliberately with conscious focus and intention on it. Maybe unbeknownst to you, you've been manifesting things all your life. You just didn't call it that. You did not realize the results in your life are there because they are what you were in alignment with, whether negative or positive.

This condition is all about acknowledging and celebrating the manifestations, big and small.

Do you normally find you accomplish one task or goal, or have a desire of yours met and then just move on to the next thing? There is no acknowledging yourself or celebrating your success. Forgetting to reward yourself with some sort of praise is easy to do, especially if you are a task-oriented person.

Or, maybe you move on to the next thing without ever feeling fully complete with it, because it seemed as though it was not producing the results you were hoping to achieve.

It's far too rare for us to take time to acknowledge ourselves. Think about that. What if it were a friend you were helping in some way? Every day, you were helping your friend to move in the right direction in her life and stay connected to her thoughts and feelings, and she was starting to realize success. Big and small things were happening for her. Her social life was improving. She got a small raise at work. She was receiving rewards and getting asked out to lunch more often. You noticed, but she never mentioned a thing about it to you. No thank you or acknowledgement of her blessings.

Would you keep guiding her?

After a while, you would probably disconnect with this friend or stop offering your guidance.

This is a good comparison to what happens when we fail to recognize or acknowledge our own manifestations. Failure to celebrate the manifestations can prevent you from receiving further guidance. You'll have to exert more energy to achieve things, or just stop manifesting your desires all together.

Perhaps you are still working toward a larger, more important desire to manifest. However, along the way to the result you want to create, there are plenty of smaller manifestations happening daily.

It's important you take time to recognize and honor the big and small manifestations, the results, the successes you have already achieved, along the way to the fulfillment of your major desires.

What Have You Already Manifested in Your Life?

Be sure to list your manifestations every day. When you look at those things and want the things in your life you already do have, you are observing something positive, rather than something negative. By doing this, you are bound to create even more of the good stuff which is already happening.

Maybe you're in a situation right now where your desire has taken a turn and you're not happy with how things are unfolding. Instead of thinking you have failed, or you haven't succeeded, you could choose to look at this as the universe's funny way of pointing you in the direction of something even better. What results **have** you achieved? Have you learned something new? Have you developed new resources, new relationships? Has anything improved?

Every day is an opportunity to look at what you have with appreciation.

Take a moment to assess your results. Where are you now in relationship to your desire?

Have you achieved it fully?

If you feel complete with it, take time to embrace it, acknowledge it, and thank the universe and yourself for helping you. Reward yourself. Give yourself the gift of self-care, a special treat you've been wanting, a day off, a night out, or time with your favorite person or pet.

What are you going to do now that you've fulfilled one desire?

To come in alignment with this condition, you need to acknowledge your results and celebrate your success.

If you are still working on manifesting a certain desire, you may be wondering if it's going to show up.

Signs Your Manifestation is Near

The universe is always giving you help, but it's easy to miss the signs (especially when they come in unexpected ways). When you start to acknowledge and receive signs from the universe, the universe will give you more of what you want and continue guiding and leading you toward the fulfillment of your desire.

Here are some examples of signs which may indicate that your manifestation is near:

- You hear about it everywhere—tv, radio, conversations, online, and offline.
- You feel happier for no reason.

- Things are getting easier.
- People offer to help you.
- You receive invitations to relevant events.
- The object of your desire appears in dreams.
- You start meeting new people.
- You find yourself in new territory.
- Unexplainable coincidences are taking place.
- You have an abundance of energy and motivation.
- Repetitive patterns begin showing up such as numbers, shapes, symbols, colors, words, pictures.
- Your sleep improves because you feel more relaxed, less stress.
- Things that used to bother you no longer do.
- You receive gifts and favors out of the blue.
- Oddly, you can also see obstacles. If everything else seems right, except for the one big obstacle, this could mean it is time to revisit and release a limiting belief in order to fully move forward.

Have you noticed any specific signs your desire is on its way? Study the list above and take some time to write down what signs you are experiencing. Can you come up with some others, not on the list that are entirely unique to your situation?

Celebrate Your Success

A good way to get started with this step is to write down the evidence in a journal at the end of the day.

Make sure to include anything that happened to you during the day that moved you a little bit closer to your goal.

There are many small successes along the way toward your ideal outcome or your desire.

Let's take the case of Emma, who wants to manifest a successful six-figure online coaching business. After spending 45 minutes with a potential client on a discovery call, her prospect does not take her offer and sign up for her coaching package. Ordinarily, this situation might be viewed in a negative light.

On a positive side, Emma can think of the other 5 discovery calls she had that week, which is a significant improvement. Every discovery call that does not commit to coaching gets her one step closer to one that closes the deal. This awareness also allows her to work on improving her skills. She's had a great opportunity to connect with a person and possibly help them shift a perspective. The prospect is coming away having a positive experience and now they are carrying a positive thought about Emma.

Sam, in his pursuit of his soulmate, has made several new connections. He's gone out on two dates. He received compliments at dinner on how well-spoken he is. This has helped boost his confidence. He takes this as a sign that, even though he has not found the right one just yet, she is right around the corner.

Exercise #1: Celebrate your Manifestations

Time: 10 minutes
Worksheet Available: Celebrate the Manifestations
Download your worksheet at:http://www.VictoriaMGallagher.com/ploabook

Write in a daily manifestation diary. List at least one positive thing every day that is leading you toward the fulfillment of your desire.

Section 4: The Qualities

We must become the change we want to see.

- Mahatma Gandhi

I will now go over the top qualities you need to develop to become a more natural manifester.

These qualities will help clear your energy and give you more power toward your manifesting efforts.

They will also help you improve your connection with superconscious and increase the rate of frequency of your energy vibration.

The qualities are not mere suggestions. They are prerequisites if you want maximum manifesting power.

As you work toward developing these qualities within yourself, you will raise your level of awareness and attract more of what you want, versus what you don't want.

To improve these qualities, I suggest that you prioritize the ones from weakest to strongest and begin to strengthen the ones where you are weak.

For each of the qualities you wish to improve, in addition to any exercises mentioned, I recommend downloading the suggested meditation script. Record it and listen for a minimum period of 30 days for best results.

Or, you may find it easier to simply upgrade to my professionally recorded version of these meditations.

Quality #1 Attitude

What attitude are you experiencing right now? Most people tend not to think about their attitude. If this is you, think about it right now. Your attitude is everything and it also determines your success.

Your attitude influences how you perceive whatever is happening in your life. It also determines how everything in life perceives you.

Knowledge, skills, and attitude are the three major elements required to become successful at anything you pursue in your life, including how you approach making Law of Attraction work for you or against you. They are fundamental for success.

Knowledge is information. Everyone has access to all the information they can ingest. Skill is an ability. Anyone can train themselves and become skilled at practically anything. Your attitude, however, affects how you interact with knowledge and skills. If you have a bad attitude, how much are you going to learn? How difficult will it be for you to develop a new skill? How will you apply your skills and knowledge?

These questions reveal the answer of why attitude is the most important quality to develop to help achieve your greatest potential in life.

Choose to develop an attitude which attracts success toward you.

Even a simple thought expressed several times throughout each day such as *"I know something wonderful is going to happen to me today,"* creates an energy of positive expectancy and retrains your automatic thinking. Though you cannot always change your circumstances, if you change your attitude you will change your life. Each of these qualities I'll be discussing are an attitude you can choose to embrace if you desire it.

As you go through each of the next chapters in this section, make an honest query. Have you sincerely developed this quality within yourself? Or does it require further improvement?

The Law of Attraction comes down to your attitude toward it. Given that you get what you think about most often. If you have a negative attitude, it's generally going to be matched with more things to have a negative attitude about.

You may find yourself in the presence of others who have a negative attitude. Though you cannot change them, you can choose to non-judgingly disengage from the negativity. Most often, people are negative when they are thinking about the opposite of what they want. They may feel powerless to do anything about their situation. You could ask a question that interrupts their negative thought pattern by simply asking them what they would prefer instead.

One way to not allow another's pessimism to penetrate your positive vibration is to hold a feeling of compassion for them. They have not yet learned how their thoughts are affecting their reality. If they are unwilling to change their negative attitude, it's very likely you'll simply find yourself less motivated to share space with them and you'll be attracted to people who have an attitude which is more of a match.

Finally, don't always expect yourself to have a perfectly positive attitude. That is unrealistic; however, maintaining awareness of your thoughts and feelings is realistic. You will find you fluctuate, but you can always do your best and improve with practice.

Download *Have a Great Attitude Meditation Script* at: http://www.VictoriaMGallagher.com/ploabook

Quality #2 Awareness

"To have greater self-awareness or understanding means to have a better grasp of reality."

- Dalai Lama

Self-awareness is the most important aspect of personal development. It determines nearly everything else, including whether you're able to stay motivated and achieve your goals. The only person you can change is yourself. When you choose to transform your life, you'll notice changes in your environment, including the people who surround you. The world is your mirror and both the negative and positive situations you encounter are created by you.

The journey of self-discovery is never-ending. It requires courage to peel away layers of deeply held beliefs. You'll discover wonderful things about yourself when you simply become more aware. You learn from your mistakes as well as the mistakes of others.

When you become self-aware, you know your strengths, weaknesses, and personality type. But it's more than this. Fully knowing yourself includes being aware of your thoughts and watching them objectively as an observer, without emotion or attachment.

While it's easy for us to think of our good qualities, our negative traits are often pushed aside. You may even find justifications for your negative thoughts and behaviors. One way to cultivate awareness is to look deep into yourself and examine all your characteristics, positive and negative.

Self-awareness entails observing your thoughts and actions. One of the best ways to do this is by writing in a journal every day.

Keeping a journal will help you see the patterns and values that are helping or hindering you.

Self-Awareness Exercise: Journal on the following subjects. Write at least a page on each one.

- Your goals.
- The events, thoughts, and beliefs that make you happy or sad.
- Your strengths and weaknesses.
- Your values and beliefs.
- Your philosophy on life.
- Your achievements, how you accomplished them, and what you learned from them.
- Your failures, how they came about, and how to prevent them from recurring.
- How you relate to others.

- How you see yourself and others.

The rewards of self-awareness are profound and will help you create the life of your dreams.

Download *Journey Toward Self-Awareness Meditation Script* at:http://www.VictoriaMGallagher.com/ploabook

Quality #3 Balance

Why is finding balance essential for raising your vibration?

Life is all about balance. It is easy to get caught up and overwhelmed with daily priorities, either at work or at home. It's a common conflict. When you spend an excessive amount of energy on one aspect of life, others may suffer.

Being out of balance often leads to stress and anxiety. Too much time spent at work leaves less time for relaxation and hobbies at home, and vice versa.

You don't have to choose one area of your life over the other. You shouldn't. Each aspect is equally important for your personal growth and to become a more well-rounded person.

I've personally experienced how difficult it can be to keep up with fitness at the same time as career goals. However, since I have recently brought both areas into balance, I find that both are expanding beautifully.

Each part of yourself works in harmony with the other, making the other that much better. When you are balanced, you are centered and peaceful. Therefore, you feel good. You are naturally attuned, and more intuitive. You have a clearer signal with the signs the universe is sending you.

What can you do to achieve balance in your life?

Think of yourself as a person who has four quadrants.

Take a moment to consider, 1 being weaker and 10 being stronger, how would you rank yourself in each of these four areas?

Physical - Your health, fitness, being active. _____

Ask: *What are some ways to get healthy? (Taking the stairs, walking, aerobics class, etc.)*

Emotional - Your feelings, your relationships, your enjoyment. _____

Ask: *What are some things I can do each day to nurture my personal relationships?*

Mental - Your career, intellect, and learning. _____

Ask: *Do you feel you spend too much, or too little time and energy focused on work? What are the action steps you can take to reduce or increase focus on your work?*

Spiritual - Your connection with yourself, your higher self, nature, and the world at large. _____

Ask: *What can you do to strengthen your spiritual connection?*

After ranking yourself on all four sides, identify the areas that need strengthening. Ask yourself the strengthening questions. Allocate some of your time and energy to getting that part of you more into alignment with the rest of you.

As you practice moderation in each area of your life, you find your life functions smoother. You'll feel more in alignment in each essential area. It takes practice, but it's a practice well worth pursuing.

A balanced life is a peaceful life in harmony with the universe.

Download *Balance Your Life Meditation Script* at: http://www.VictoriaMGallagher.com/ploabook

Quality #4 Compassion

One of the best kept secrets to raising your vibration is compassion.

In Buddhism, *the supreme state* is characterized by boundless wisdom and infinite compassion.

At times, we find ourselves living in a world that seems to view compassion as a sign of weakness, whereas wisdom is a sign of strength. However, anything which makes you happier and relieves the suffering of others is most certainly a strength. Strengthening your sense of compassion will make you feel very good about yourself and is useful in serving others better.

Focusing on helping others is a fast and powerful way to make yourself feel better. Even small acts of kindness promote a healthy sense of self-esteem.

It's easy to get caught up in your own experiences. However, when you divert your attention from your own problems, and focus on putting yourself in someone else's shoes, your problems seem less significant.

How to Practice Compassion

- Notice when someone is hurting or getting overwhelmed. You can train yourself to view others' unpleasant situations without judgment and with a calm mind.

- Put yourself in the other person's position. It can be difficult to feel compassionate during an argument. Try to take the other person's perspective. Look beyond any feelings of hostility. Seek common ground and opportunities for compromise.

- Listen carefully and respectfully. Even if you hold different views and disagree with someone else's thinking, you can still listen to them with an open mind. Hear what they are saying from their perspective. You don't have to agree with a person to empathize with them.

- Focus on their good qualities. Often, we naturally feel compassion for people we love. By noticing their positive attributes, you will increase your feelings of warmth toward them.

- Offer to help when appropriate. Sometimes you can ask people specifically what you can do to be of service. From time to time, you can help by simply providing someone with companionship and a listening ear.

- Volunteer your time. This could be at an animal shelter, a women's shelter, a senior center or some other cause you care about. Spending even one hour a week, devoted toward outwardly focused activities is a sure-fire way to develop a feeling of compassion.

Compassion will improve your life and deepen your happiness, which of course increases the quality of your vibration. When you reach out to others, you feel better about yourself. It helps you take the focus off things that might be bothering you in your own life and fills you with love and satisfaction for extending your kindness and caring attitude toward a person in need.

Download *Compassion Meditation Script* at:
http://www.VictoriaMGallagher.com/ploabook

Quality #5 Confidence

Are you struggling with doubts which hold you back from reaching your dreams? Do you feel nervous pursuing activities that would lead to your success?

Whatever the cause of lack of self-confidence, you likely struggle to believe you deserve the good things in life you're trying to use the Law of Attraction to manifest.

Confidence is much easier than you might think. You were created for a purpose, and you're the only one who can fulfill that purpose.

You have a lot to offer the world. All you need is to discover the passion inside of you and step out of your comfort zone and go get it.

Ask yourself the following questions.

- What would you dare to attempt if you knew it was impossible for you to fail?
- What are your dreams?
- What have you always wanted to do?
- What are your talents?
- What abilities have you received compliments on?
- What are you excited about in your life right now?
- What's great about your life?

Myths About Confidence

Myth 1: Success is necessary for confidence. Although success may give you a confidence boost, it's not a requirement to have it.

You can have confidence without success. As a matter of fact, you need to develop confidence to become a success.

To develop confidence, take note of all your good qualities and any achievements you do have, no matter how big or small.

Even small habits, making your bed daily for example, will cause you to develop confidence.

Begin by committing to check off 5 or 10 small daily tasks every day and your confidence will grow as a result.

Myth 2: Only extroverts can be confident.

Being an extrovert or an introvert has nothing to do with confidence. There are many extroverts who aren't confident. You can be an introvert and still have high confidence levels. It's not necessary to need to be the center of attention.

Confidence is an internal experience. Accept and embrace the reality of your true nature and confidence is a natural aftereffect.

Myth 3: You have to be confident all the time. This is practically impossible, as confidence levels do go up and down. Trying new things or being fearful of something are two examples of when your confidence level could shift.

Plus, you don't have to be confident every hour of every day. Your confidence levels will fluctuate depending on your mood, your health, your accomplishments, and a variety of other events.

Touch base with yourself, regardless of how confident you are feeling. Ask yourself what is generating this feeling. See if you can notice a pattern with times when you are feeling less confident and do less of that. Conversely, notice if there is a pattern you can model to build upon those times when you are most confident.

Download *Developing Greater Self-Confidence Meditation Script* at: http://www.VictoriaMGallagher.com/ploabook

Quality #6 Consistency

Consistency is a major predictor of success in any endeavor.

One key to getting better results with anything in life is consistency. Think about anything you've ever tried to achieve, such as getting in better shape or clearing your mind. If you were trying to lose weight, how effective would you be at that if you only dieted and exercised sporadically or occasionally? The results would not be favorable.

Similarly, if you wanted to begin a meditation practice, but you only practice it one time per week and at different times of the day, it's not going to have a chance to take root and have any sort of impact on your mindset.

What you do occasionally doesn't impact your life significantly. A small positive step forward each day adds up to something positive over time.

Use the power of consistency to enhance your success.

An effective way to predict your success is to examine your average day and project the likely outcome into the future. 20 minutes each morning spent practicing yoga will yield better far better results than practicing it for 2 hours on Saturday and not again for the rest of the week.

Consider all your daily habits and behaviors. Are your consistent actions the ones that are going to produce financial, emotional, physical, and spiritual success?

Realize many changes are like seeds being planted in your garden. You don't plant the seed and suddenly see a tree the next day. It takes time before the first signs begin showing up.

You must water the soil where the seed was planted every day, consistently.

When you plant a new habit, you need to do a little each day before that habit takes root and begins to grow. It may already be starting to grow, but you can't see it just yet. But with consistency you will one day notice your plans have materialized.

Consistency Exercise:

Think about one thing in your life you gave up on. How consistent were you in taking daily actions to get that thing? Did you give up on it too soon? What would happen if you took on a consistent action toward that goal every day for the next 30 days, 60 days, or even 90 days?

You might be thinking, *90 Days? Wow! That's a long time, Victoria!*

But, is it? Most people stop short on achieving success because they fail to realize that while it may take 21 days to form a habit, it takes 2 months to 8 months to fully integrate a lifestyle change.

Do you want to improve your life? Or would you rather complain that it's not improving fast enough?

What is one lifestyle habit you are willing to have a breakthrough in over the next 90 days?

This book has plenty of options to consider, many which would make a dramatic change in your level of happiness, satisfaction, and success in your life.

Download *Consistency Meditation Script* at:
http://www.VictoriaMGallagher.com/ploabook

Quality #7 Charisma

Let's talk about naturally attractive people. I'm not talking about people who are simply good looking, either. A person can be an infamous *"ten"* in good looks yet give off negative energy with things like a bad attitude, selfishness, arrogance, dishonesty, and meanness that they are a complete turn off to others.

Attractiveness is not about appearance, intelligence, status, or wealth. It's about personality.

What does it mean to have a charismatic personality?

Everyone knows charisma when they're around it. It can be a bit challenging to put your finger on it, but *"there's just something about them."* Charismatic people are those who have something about them you want, and it feels wonderful to be around. They tend to lead successful lives because they have a way with people. It's easier for them to get what they want because people are enticed by whatever they are talking about.

There are few characteristics that will increase your vibration more than a high level of charisma. Luckily this is a quality everyone can foster.

Here are a few ways to develop charisma:

Being present with others

Think about the charismatic people you know. Aren't they fully engaged with you when you're speaking? They make you feel like you're the most fascinating person in the room.

Maintaining your focus and listening intently are great ways to accomplish this. Have you ever watched Tony Robbins in a conversation? Next time you do, take note of the high level of attention he gives each person he interacts with. You can't help but to fall in love with the way he works with a person. His skill and magnetic quality come from his masterful ability to be present and listen. As such, he can create almost instant transformation. The intense focus he offers an individual allows him to tap into the exact message that person needs in order to rise above whatever issue they came to him with.

Body language

Otherwise known as non-verbal communication, your body is communicating to others all the time and at an unconscious level.

You may be communicating one thing with your words. However, you are communicating much more than you realize by the mere tone of your voice. Do you make eye contact? Are your arms crossed or open? There is a whole study about body language, and I have created a course to help people develop better body language as well as learn to decode the body language of others.

You can find my program online at:
http://www.bodylanguageadvantage.com.

Ultimately, people who are charismatic have body language which is congruent with the words they are speaking.

Charisma is simply attraction mixed with personal power. It's a high level of authenticity mixed with taking the focus off what others think about you and putting the focus on them. It's about caring about others and making them feel amazingly good about themselves.

Download *Be Charismatic Meditation Script* at:
http://www.VictoriaMGallagher.com/ploabook

Quality #8 Creativity

You are already creative by your inherent nature. Every single person on the planet was created by a creator and imbued with the same power to create. To the degree with which you experience yourself as a creator is the degree you will experience the positive side of The Law of Attraction.

Creativity is an energy flow, which is enhanced by positive emotions and being in alignment with who you are.

There are times when we all want to be more creative. We wish that there was something we could do to express ourselves and create something beautiful at the same time.

If you're looking for ways to discover your creative side and release the artist within, here are a few simple activities that you can do to get the creative energy flowing.

Express your creative self

Set aside *"me time"* to allow creativity to flow through you freely.

In the book, **The Artists Way** by Julia Cameron, she suggests you take yourself out at least one time a week for what's called an artist's date.

The artists date is a time for you to express your creative side and even though the actual activity may be completely unrelated to the ways you need to realize more creativity in your life, taking time to be artistic helps you overcome deeper feelings of shame, which may remain buried inside you about your creative side.

Try on new ways of expressing yourself

Here are a few ideas to allow the creativity to flow through you.

Paint – Even if you don't know how to paint you can go to a painting class or buy a paint by numbers set.

Dance – This is a great way to literally move some energy out of your body. You can do it alone when no one is watching, or out at a night club where you can feed off the energy of the crowd and learn new ways to move your body.

Sing – Something about singing just makes you feel alive. Again, you can spend time alone singing to your favorite songs or brave it and go out for some karaoke!

Write – Writing helps stimulate new ideas. The best way to write for creativity is to physically use a pen and paper. Commit to write for a specific amount of time, or a specific number of pages. Just write whatever comes to mind even if it makes no sense.

Increasing your creativity starts in small, simple ways. Your life is filled with opportunities for you to test your creative energies, but it's up to you to act!

You hold the creative keys to bring all your desires to fruition. By allowing your mind some time to run free, you will find new ideas come to you that you may have never connected with previously.

Most importantly, believe you are creative. Do the activities and you will prove to yourself you are.

What will you do this week to stimulate your creativity?

Download *Expand Creativity and Imagination Meditation Script* at: http://www.VictoriaMGallagher.com/ploabook

Quality #9 Flexibility

Being flexible plays a huge role in manifesting your dreams. It can be a challenge; however, you'll find flexibility is paramount to finding success. When you are flexible, you are the opposite of rigid and set in your own ways. Flexibility indicates openness and an ability to go with the flow, when necessary.

If you're stuck and haven't been able to manifest, you may be clinging to a desire to control things. Remember, the how is not your domain. How things show up is typically far off from how you originally thought they would. Because of this, you must learn to accept the new course of action readily, so you do not stall your manifestations.

Why Is Flexibility A Key to Success?

Being flexible opens your thinking up to new opportunities you may never have thought about on your own, had you not been nudged in their direction.

Flexibility helps you re-organize your schedule when something unexpected happens without the change creating unnecessary stress and anxiety. This could be as simple as taking a detour when a road is closed without neither complaining nor worry. Or it could be when a work project presents an obstacle that takes you on a new, unanticipated path—one which could lead to even more success.

How Can You Become More Flexible?

Notice your immediate thoughts and reactions to change.

An example might be complaining about a last-minute change of plans. This wasn't something you planned for! Keep the big picture in mind and let go of the small details.

Get out of your comfort zone.

In order to become more flexible, you'll need to get used to regularly stepping out of your comfort zone. It may help to start with small things because it won't be as much of a shock if you're a routine person.

Expect change.

Change is a law of nature. Why try to fight it? Anticipate things will change and you'll be much happier in the end. Be prepared to shift yourself to adapt to situations. Look at it as a sign that the universe is trying to point you in the right direction.

Keeping an open mind gives you the power to face daily challenges.

When you are willing to adapt to new conditions, you'll continue to make progress even when unexpected situations come your way.

Questions for Self-Reflection on Flexibility:

1. In what situations have you become better off because you were willing to be flexible?

2. What ways of thinking makes being flexible easier?

3. What ways of thinking makes being flexible more of a challenge?

Download *Flexibility Meditation Script* at:
http://www.VictoriaMGallagher.com/ploabook

Quality #10 Focus

As you've surely figured out by now, focus is one of the main keys everyone thinks of when it comes to attracting what you want with the Law of Attraction.

Focus on what you want, not on what you don't want. What you think about, you become. It's a pretty simple concept, right?

While the concept may be simple to understand in theory, the actual practice of focusing on what you want can present challenges. Not all people have trained their brains to recognize when they are starting to think about things they don't want. It's so easy to get sucked into negative thinking because it's all around us.

Creating a mindset that is disciplined to think only about what you do want is going to take some time, dedication, and patience with yourself. You're not always going to be perfect at this. And that's okay.

I want you to understand this. Consciously and deliberately focusing on what you do want is a rare quality. And it's the number one reason I believe people fail at creating the life of their dreams with Law of Attraction. The world is full of negativity. Do you ever turn on the news? Even though pessimism is everywhere, you can choose to change your focus and create your own reality.

Luckily, I've set myself up to mostly be in a controlled environment. I work alone in my house. I rarely have to put up with traffic, or other people's conversations. I have set my Facebook newsfeed even to filter out anyone who loves to complain. I can escape most of the negativity. Matter of fact, when someone starts complaining to me about their day it surprises me now. It's not a conversation I'm accustomed to having. Then I'm reminded, *oh yes, people are still doing that to themselves.*

These opportunities become ones where I can invite someone into a discussion about the Law of Attraction. Perhaps offer them insight into how they can overcome the bad habit of drawing in more negative things to their lives.

You might look at me and say, *"You're out of touch with reality. Don't you care about what's happening in the world?"*

My answer to this is that I choose to focus on what makes me feel good and on what I have control over. I don't have any control over things that have already come to pass, which is what you learn about by staying in touch with the news.

I do have compassion for those people who experience injustices. And in my one-on-one work with people, I am easily able to jump into their shoes and see life through their eyes and feel the empathy for what they are experiencing.

Simply put, I choose not to focus on data that isn't in alignment with keeping a high vibration toward what I desire in life. And it works. I can also do more to help others with meaningful changes by adhering to this practice.

My mission is to cause a shift in people's awareness from one of powerlessness to one of personal empowerment. As such, maintaining my *"feel good"* state allows me to do what is within my power and that is helping make people happy. If I can help make more people feel happy, then I am creating the news I want to see in the world. That is my mission and it remains the same regardless of past events. It's about creating a better future I envision for myself and everyone on the planet. I like waking people up and expanding their awareness, so they can help themselves take control over their life, feel better about themselves, and improve their chances at having a happy and successful life.

Now, you may currently be living a life that is less than optimal and not how you thought it would be since childhood. For you, that might mean you are struggling financially or maybe you are feeling lonely because you just got divorced or you haven't met your soulmate. You know these things are true right now because you see the evidence of your situations all around you. You see your low bank balance, or the bills piling up, or the piece-of-junk car sitting in your parking spot. You see the empty side of the bed, or that no one is sitting across from you at the dinner table.

That real evidence, just like the evidence of what's happening in the world on the news, could make you feel depressed if you choose to focus your attention on those realities.

How you choose to observe your reality effects your vibration. When you change your perspective and appreciate and focus on what you do have, the law of attraction responds by giving you more of what you are focused on.

In other words, are you complaining about what you don't want or what you don't have?

Switch Your Focus:

It's time to switch your focus and create your own news, if you will.

Set an alarm on your phone to remind you every hour or every half hour to ask yourself, what am I focusing on?

Ask yourself:

Are you focused on creating an abundance mindset or are you focused on continuing to live in the reality of lack?

Are you focused on your problems or are you focused on your solutions?

What are your conversations about most of the time?

Do you find yourself talking about what others have and feeling jealous you don't have the same things?

Here's an opportunity to just observe the very thing you want. Realize if it's possible for someone else to have that, then it's totally possible for you to, as well. Do you see how different that way of focusing on it is?

Train yourself to talk about, think about, and see in your reality the life you want to experience.

Download *Stay Focused on Your Highest Priorities Meditation Script* at: http://www.VictoriaMGallagher.com/ploabook

Quality #11 Forgiveness

What does forgiveness have to do with Law of Attraction?

When you are holding on to grudges or not letting go of the past, you are anchoring yourself to the past. It's most important for you to understand this energy you carry around of not letting go has a negative vibration.

You can get used to this cumbersome weight just enough that you barely detect it. Yet, you can't quite figure out why you don't resonate with your dreams and your goals.

Resentment keeps you in a low vibration that will surely keep you stuck right where you are and prevent you from moving forward in your life.

It's not easy to let go of an event that hurt you. Forgiving the person or situation charged with that event is difficult, especially because you likely feel wronged in some way. It might seem as though you're letting them off the hook somehow or making whatever they did okay.

However, forgiveness is not something you do for them. It is something you to for yourself!

The other person has most likely moved on and does not even care if you forgive them. You forgive others, so YOU can free yourself of the negative energy around an event and enjoy your life again as you did before.

I like to use the term, to give as before. In other words, after you forgive them, you'll go back to the way things were again. Of course, in extreme cases where actual abuse took place, you would likely not continue your relationship with this person. Still, in your own mind, you will free yourself of your own burden of carrying it around, wishing bad things to happen to them, and rehashing the old memory.

Exercise: Forgiveness Strategies

1. Understand what forgiveness means. Some people believe forgiveness means making what the other person did okay or acceptable. You can forgive someone and still make the decision to never speak to them again. Forgiveness simply means you're not going to dwell on the situation anymore. You've decided to not feel bad about it any longer. You're moving on with your life and letting go of the past.

2. Accept the past can never be changed. You can't undo what has been done. There's no way to completely erase what happened. The only way you can be whole and complete and feel good again is to forgive.

3. What do you believe you're gaining from not forgiving? Are you punishing the other person? Do you believe your resentment somehow impacts that person? Most likely they've moved on with their life, and you deserve to, as well. You will get to move on when you choose to let it go for good and stop resenting something that happened in the past.

4. Understand the cost of not forgiving. What is it costing you to maintain your feelings of resentment? Is it preventing you from enjoying your life? Are you unable to have another relationship? Are you losing sleep? Do you feel lingering negative emotions blocking your positive vibrations all day? Withholding your forgiveness is not free. The one who pays the price is you.

5. Think about the benefits you'll get when you choose to forgive. If you were not feeling resentment, anger, or sadness, what feelings would you have instead? Would you feel peace? Freedom. What else might you experience?

6. Forgive. Just do it. Make the decision and let it go. Here, I suggest either visualizing yourself having a conversation with them and setting them free, wanting peace, happiness, love, and freedom for them. Then, literally see them with those emotional states. It's a very powerful technique.

7. Learn the lesson. What can you take away from the situation? Whenever there's a hurt, there's usually a lesson to be learned. What would you do differently?

Feel the freedom and watch your energy vibe go way up, allowing you to bring in good things into that place where you were stuck before.

Download *Forgiveness Forest Meditation Script* at: http://www.VictoriaMGallagher.com/ploabook

Quality #12 Integrity

Talk is cheap! It's an expression we use to describe a situation that it's much easier said than done. This common expression implies you don't believe the person is going to fulfill on their promise.

Unfortunately, it's all too common to say one thing and act another way. And this is regarded as a normal, rational way of being. People break their word with each other all the time and flippantly apologize (repeatedly) as if the person they broke their word with is the one suffering the consequences.

Let's define integrity. Many people think of the definition of integrity in terms of morality. Doing the right thing. And while living with integrity by its very nature will inherently have you doing *"the right thing,"* integrity means something greater.

Integrity comes from the root word, integer, which means a whole number; a number that is not a fraction and a thing which is complete.

So, let's use the definition of whole and complete.

What does it mean to be whole and complete? And why is this quality important for attracting things into your life?

For many years I have been a student of **Landmark Education**. They put integrity into the context of honoring your word as yourself. I very much subscribe to this theory—your integrity is about the power of your word.

Your word is you. Your word is your power. Your word is your ability to create, to be effective, and to be trustworthy.

Let's talk about trustworthy…

Think about something you heavily rely on, perhaps your car.

How much do you trust your car to get you where you need to go?

If your car is missing any parts or resources such as fuel, it's just not going to function at optimal levels.

The car is not whole and complete. The car is out of integrity.

Let's compare that with your word. You might think making a promise to yourself to work out tomorrow or telling your friend you'll call them at 1:00PM is quite trivial. However, when you don't hold those agreements you are breaking your word, not only with the other person, but with yourself.

It's the same thing. The power of your word has just ticked down a notch. You're no longer whole and complete with your word.

When you fail to honor your word, you are undermining and diminishing yourself because you are less than whole and complete. Not only do you appear untrustworthy to others, but you're now vulnerable to no longer being able to trust yourself.

And yet, it's almost universally accepted and rationalized to not even acknowledge it, when we break our word. Excuses are made, and we are off the hook.

I suggest we are not off the hook. There's simply no way to quantify the damage that is done when you don't keep your word.

If you did exactly what you said you would do 100% of the time, how much power would you have?

How much more effective would you be at creating your life?

What if you always did go to the gym the next day when you said you would—100% of the time? That would be the norm. It would be odd for you not to do it. It would be out of character. You just know you are doing it because you said you would. There would be no question, whatsoever, about whether your word about going to the gym would cause you to go to the gym or not.

How would other areas of your life be impacted? When you always act upon your word, then your word is creating your reality. When you fail to act according to your word, then you are at the mercy of whatever life throws your way. You're not the one controlling and effectuating change.

Now, just like the car situation, cars can be restored back to their whole and complete state again. They can become reliable, trustworthy again. They can become good as new. The amount of work required to get the car back to whole and complete again, depends upon how much out of integrity they are.

The same holds true with your integrity. You can restore yourself back to a pure, innocent, whole, and complete person. Once again, you will have a blank canvass for creating your life exactly as you say.

Integrity goes even beyond your spoken agreements. It's about authentically valuing yourself and your personal values in life.

What do you value most in your life?

Think about this question for a moment. Say that one of your top values is your health.

Now let's look. Is the way you are living your life in alignment with that value? Are you living your life, as if that area is most important to you? The truth is mirrored back to you and will suggest what is important.

What are you putting up with?

If your health is your number one value in life, then why do you allow yourself to weigh more than your ideal weight? Why are you not exercising, going to the doctor, dealing with a health issue that could easily be corrected and eating way too much sugar?

It gets brought back to word, the power to create. You are saying one thing and doing another. You say health is important to you, but you are allowing yourself to treat your body like it's not. That's a misalignment.

The power of your word influences your neural pathways in your brain. Your word being in or out of alignment influences the energy field all around you and the power you have to co-create with universal intelligence.

It's quite confusing to the subconscious and superconscious when your words and actions don't match. Yet we all do it. We just accept the little white lies we tell each other and tell ourselves. It's ok if you're *"just a little bit"* out of integrity. *"It's normal,"* *"It's realistic,"* *"People do it all the time,"* *"Don't make a big deal out of it."* Ha!

Yes, it IS very normal. And if a normal life is what you want, then, you're exactly right. it's not a big deal.

But, if you want to live an extraordinary life, or to at least intentionally change the one you have so you can feel happier, then it's a very big deal.

The deeper levels of mind don't look at the size of the word you broke with yourself. When words and actions don't line up, it chips away at your true, pure, innocent nature. Your original state of being.

You came to this world with a blank canvas, a nothingness of pure untainted and extraordinary power and potential. From that place of wholeness, there are no doubts, no fears, no bad habits, no limitations.

A blank canvas is empty. It's clean and unmarked. It's ready to be made into something.

You can wipe the slate clean, strengthen the power of your word, and become a clear channel for manifestation.

To gain powerful access to create the world you dream of will require you to restore yourself to integrity.

Here's the simplest way to do it:

Restore Integrity

As soon as you know you are not going to do what you said, which includes the way you said you would or the way someone is expecting you to, you communicate. You make a new promise and keep the new promise.

By adopting this one very simple practice, you have honored your word.

Here's an example. You agreed to meet your friend at 1:00PM for lunch. At 12:00PM, something happened which is more than likely going to make you late for your lunch date. You could try to make it, speed through traffic (which is breaking the agreement with the traffic laws you signed when you got your driver's license) and arrive frazzled and stressed at 15 minutes after the hour and explain to your friend, who was on time and has now spent time waiting for you. You'll explain what happened. Your friend will say, *"Okay, that's okay."* (When it's not okay, but she's now feeling the need to tell that little white lie to not make things awkward between you.)

To restore integrity in this situation, all that you would need to do is simply call your friend at that moment when you found out something is going to cause you to be late. You don't need to even explain it. You can simply mention something happened and I need to renegotiate what time we meet. *"I can arrive at 1:15PM. Is that okay with you?"* And then, you keep your promise to arrive at 1:15PM. Integrity restored!

Integrity does not mean perfection. Unforeseen events are going to happen. Plans change. Not acknowledging when your original agreement changed and pretending like nothing happened creates unspoken negative energy.

Life is easier when you live with integrity. Restoring yourself to act with integrity is as difficult as changing any habit would be at first. However, the more you act with integrity, the easier your life steadily becomes.

As you act with integrity in everything you do, you will find every part of your life will improve. You will begin to attract the best people and situations.

Download *Living with Integrity Meditation Script* at: http://www.VictoriaMGallagher.com/ploabook

Quality #13 Motivation

Why is being motivated a critical component of improving your vibration?

Motivation is what causes you to do anything. Everything we do in our life happens because we are motivated to do it, be it get out of bed in the morning, eat, walk out the door, or pursue our desires in life and make them a reality.

If you don't have any motivation to act, the universe recognizes that as a sign you are not passionate about your desire.

What is motivation?

Motivation comes from things you want, desire, or need. It stimulates you to take action.

It's the driving force.

In order to feel motivated, you must have a desire and belief you will be able to satisfy or accomplish that desire. This is what incentivizes you, whether it be internally or externally, as a reward for your efforts.

According to Maslow theory, human beings are motivated by 5 different types of needs and one builds upon the other.

- **Physiological** – food, clothing, air, shelter.
- **Safety** – security, resources, health.
- **Social** – love, intimacy, connection, companionship.
- **Esteem** – status, accomplishment, freedom, recognition, respect.

- **Self-actualization** – the desire to develop and realize your full potential; to become all you can be.

The point of this hierarchy of needs is you're not exactly going after goals for self-actualization when you're running around with no clothes on, trying to figure out where your next meal is coming from.

If you are not feeling motivated, you need to realize it may be due to the fact you have other needs which are taking precedence.

Your most basic human need is for physical survival. If you do not have plenty of food, clothing, and shelter, then those needs are the ones you are going to be more motivated to act on. Once you have fulfilled those needs, your needs will change. You'll be motivated by the next level of needs.

Can you identify where on the Maslow scale of needs you are right now?

Making the Decision to Transform

Tony Robbins has stated that:

"Change happens in an instant."

What takes time is getting to this point. For change to happen, you need to believe you can change this very instant, and you are the one responsible for your own transformation. You can't expect others to change you, nor can you blame them if you fail to change.

Here are the steps Robbins suggests:

Step 1: Decide what you want to change in your life. Ask yourself what's preventing you from change. Remember not to focus on what you don't want, but on what you do want.

Step 2: Your desire to change should be urgent. Associate pain with not changing now and pleasure with changing now.

How to Associate Pain with not Changing.

Answer the following questions:

- What will this cost me if I don't change?

- What has it already cost me physically, spiritually, mentally, career-wise, and in my relationships?
- How has it affected my family and friends?

How to Associate Pleasure with Changing

- If I transform myself, how will it make me feel about myself?
- What will this change help me accomplish?
- How will this change make my family and friends feel?

Motivating Strategies for Acting on Your Transformational Decision

- **Do your research.** Finding out more about your subject will generate interest and motivation.

- **Reward yourself as you make progress.** Celebrate your little successes on the way. This will also bring you motivation to continue succeeding.

- **Join a community.** Working together with others who share your goals and ideals will allow you to learn from their mistakes and successes. It can also help keep your motivation burning and keep you on track.

- **Write down your goals.** According to research, people who write down their goals are far more likely to remain motivated and achieve their goals than those who merely make mental lists.

- **Don't seek perfection.** Many perfectionists give up on a task before they've even begun, because they're afraid of not being able to do a perfect job. This can lead to procrastination.

Now you have the most powerful keys to motivation. It's time to act and achieve your dreams. Begin it right now. Yes, this very moment!

Download *Motivation to Succeed Meditation Script* at: http://www.VictoriaMGallagher.com/ploabook

Quality #14 Optimism

There are two general attitudes you can hold: pessimism and optimism. Pessimists get what they think about most often and therefore usually create dissatisfying long-term results. Optimists are healthier, happier, and more successful.

Optimism creates an energy of positive expectation. You need to have optimism to succeed at Law of Attraction.

If you want to manifest success and raise your vibration, what kind of energy are you going to send? If you are sending an unpleasant, unforgiving, or judgmental vibration, you are going to draw in like situations and circumstances. When you always expect things to go wrong, chances are they will.

Conversely, in this universe where *"like attracts like,"* an optimistic attitude will yield better, more favorable results.

Optimism is simply an attitude you choose to have. Being an optimist doesn't mean you go through life completely oblivious to the world you see all around you. It's not about pretending to be okay and happy with everything all the time.

We live in a universe of dualism and balance. You can't know optimism without appreciating the occasional feelings of pessimism. You just want to be aware of times when you're thinking that way and spend only short amounts of time there.

Consider the ways in which optimism can help you succeed:

- Optimism has many benefits. Being optimistic can strengthen your physical, emotional, and mental health in ways that help you succeed.

- Optimism gives you the drive to try. Pessimists rarely want to try new things, so they don't get a chance to find success. On the other hand, optimists are willing to experiment and are more likely to succeed. You must be willing to do new things and make changes to find success.

- In both business and life, it's important to be flexible, so optimists have a higher probability of making their dreams come true. They're willing to keep fighting for their goals.

- Optimists also tend to be willing to take more risks. They're less likely to wait and see what will happen. Instead, they take the necessary actions to move ahead.

- Optimism gives you a positive focus on the future. Instead of getting hung up on the past, optimists tend to look toward the future.

- Researchers have found that thinking about the future in a positive way can increase your success. You're motivated to keep going and refuse to give up because you know better things are ahead.

- Optimism gives you perseverance. One of the reasons people don't find success is because they give up too soon.

- Optimists view challenges and roadblocks as normal parts of the process to find success. They're resilient and strong. So, they keep moving forward toward their goals.

- Businesses can fail, but optimists are willing to start over again. They're also willing to learn from their mistakes and rebuild from what they've learned.

Studies show optimists live longer, achieve more, and enjoy greater happiness and health. Even if you tend to see the glass as half empty, you can tap into these advantages.

How to instantly become more optimistic

You can complete most of these steps instantly, and a few require a little more time.

- **Smile**. Your facial muscles communicate with your brain. Putting on a smile will make you look and feel happier.

- **Count your blessings**. Gratitude reinforces optimism. Wake up each morning thinking about what you're thankful for. Write a gratitude list and post it near your desk where you can see it all day.

- **Challenge your assumptions**. Transform your self-talk by arguing the opposing side when you start to criticize yourself. Remember to run a reality check because unpleasant events tend to make a stronger impression than positive ones. The day your car broke down stands out more than all the years it worked fine.

- **Build on your strengths**. Studies also show that using your core strengths will cause you to view your future more favorably.

- **Focus on solutions**. Put your energy into overcoming challenges rather than making them a catastrophic event of what can go wrong. Needing a new car transmission will seem less overwhelming when you take your first steps to find a mechanic and adjust your budget to cover the bills.

- **Exercise**. Physical activity is good for your mind and body. A vigorous workout will brighten your outlook.

- **Practice mindfulness**. Trying to make yourself happier tends to backfire, but there is a better way. Engage fully with whatever you're doing. As you increase your awareness and act from your heart, even tedious tasks become more meaningful and rewarding.

Being more optimistic is likely to extend your life and help you to enjoy those extra years more. Optimism is a crucial part of finding success. It helps you stay motivated and determined as you work toward your goals.

Download *Develop and Optimistic Attitude Meditation Script* at: http://www.VictoriaMGallagher.com/ploabook

Quality #15 Patience

Miracles do not typically occur overnight. One of the most difficult skills we must learn is how to be patient.

Consider how it has taken years to create the life you have right now. It will most likely take some time to create a completely different reality.

I like to use the analogy of redirecting a steam ship. Even if you have never been on a steamship, you can most likely imagine the process one must go through to *"change the direction or course."* The ship must go through many different steps—it doesn't just happen. Once the new direction or course correction is set, then the ship begins to turn around. The changes will at first be subtle but before you know it, you are headed in a new direction.

Your new life will manifest in time, often more quickly and easily, if you allow yourself to be patient with the process.

In the case of manifestation, patience is indeed a virtue. Detaching from your desire becomes necessary. Tapping your foot and waiting impatiently, saying, *"Okay, I've done all this work, now where is my stuff already,"* will only make the wait seem longer.

Patience is an integral part of the manifestation process, but how can you develop it? In a world where we demand instant gratification, it is certainly a less common style of thinking.

Let's look at what patience is:

- The ability to delay gratification.
- Waiting without tension, stress, or anxiety.
- Letting go of the need for a *"quick fix."*
- Developing tolerance, compassion, and maturity.
- Gaining a sense of peace and contentment, knowing you are on the right track.
- Telling yourself good things are worth waiting for.
- Learning how to enjoy life along the way.
- Being at peace in the moment.
- Knowing you have a plan for success.

- Recognizing good things take time.

With your better understanding of patience, how can you use this quality to raise your vibration?

Here are a few things you can do:

- Detach from a specific outcome.
- Get involved in things that make you feel good.
- Know in your heart of hearts that you will manifest your desire.
- Be open to how the universe may present your desire to you.

This last bullet is an extremely important one. While it is important to be specific in what you want, we must be careful not to be too specific. Let's face it; we don't always know what's best for us. The universe often presents us with things in ways we may not have thought of or expected. It's important to maintain an open mind to remain open to bigger and better things. We must leave a little space for the universe to work its magic.

Let's look at an example:

Perhaps you have your heart set on having a certain house in a certain neighborhood, and you are very specific on the details as to how you will acquire it. What if the universe had something else, something completely different or even better in store for you? What if a situation arose where you meet the love of your life or there was a career opportunity which had you moving out of the state, or even the country for that matter, within the next several months? Then buying that house in that neighborhood would have been a huge mistake.

Now you're living in an even better neighborhood with an even better house and a new career or relationship as a bonus.

You never know what is around the corner, and if you can't learn to acquire a little patience, you may end up in the wrong place.

Let's try a little exercise called the **Alternate Reality Exercise** or the **What If Exercise**. This exercise will help you determine how open your mind is and you may end up with an entirely new perspective when it comes to developing and acquiring patience.

Alternate Reality or What If Exercise

- Focus on the desire or outcome you wish to receive.
- Ask yourself how attached you are to a specific outcome.
- Rate yourself on a scale of 1 to 10, 10 meaning you are completely open to alternate solutions and 1 meaning you are bound and determined to have one very specific thing.
- If you are anywhere from 1-5, you may need to work on opening yourself up to different possibilities. If you find yourself scoring from 6 -10, you're at a nice level of openness and patience and you'll have a much easier time allowing your desire to manifest in the best possible way.
- Practice envisioning different ways in which your desire could manifest. Take each item and list out 10 different ways in which your desire could be answered. This is a fun exercise, so make sure you open your mind up to bigger and better possibilities.

Here is a quick example:

You desire to become a famous novelist and you send out proposal after proposal, only to get rejected by publishers' time after time. What are some other ways this desire could manifest?

- You could self-publish your book.
- You could turn your book into a blog instead and gain customers by getting them hooked on the story week after week.
- Your blog could get noticed by an editor at one of the big publishing houses, and they might, in turn, ask you to write another novel.
- You could publish your book electronically and promote it with your own website.

- You could do some networking in the publishing field and make some contacts that could help you navigate the waters.

- You could win a million dollars and create your own publishing empire, only publishing novels from unknown or new authors.

I think you get the idea here. In the end, there are a million ways to make your dreams a reality, so don't get stuck on one way. By loosening your firm grip on your desire and the exact time and way it will come, you will open yourself up to a whole new world of possibilities you may have never imagined.

Download *Patience Meditation Script* at:
http://www.VictoriaMGallagher.com/ploabook

Quality #16 Responsibility

If you break down the word responsibility, it gives you one of life's clues, the instruction manual, in only two words: response ability. The ability to respond.

There are two mindsets or viewpoints you can choose as you observe the events that happen in your life.

You can perceive life is happening **TO** you. You are at the mercy of something else, outside of you. How you think, feel, react to life's circumstances are beyond your control. We shall refer to this approach as the victim mentality.

Or you can perceive life is happening **THROUGH** you. Something inside of you is the cause. You are creating, manifesting the world you see around you. How you think, feel, and act is 100% in your control. We'll call this the responsible approach.

Which approach will be most effective in manifesting your desire?

There's a comfort that comes from having an excuse for your challenges in life. Whether you can blame your issues on poor parenting, a boss that hates you, or the universe in general, it's soothing to have an excuse. However, that excuse has a cost. By putting the blame and responsibility outside yourself, you take away your power to change your situation.

Is everything your fault? Of course not. But it is your responsibility. If you don't fix it, who will? Even if you had horrible parents, there's nothing they can do about it now.

A victim mentality will keep you from living your full potential.

Do you ever feel others are always doing something to you which is holding you back?

The victim mentality can trap you in a cycle of unhappiness and pain and impact your ability to succeed at anything.

When you think you're always the victim, you avoid taking responsibility for anything. If you don't take responsibility, you also feel there's nothing you can do to resolve your challenges.

Here are some signs you've been partaking in a victim mentality.

- You feel sorry for yourself and you indulge in stories which get other people to join in on feeling sorry for you too.
- You ignore the positive factors in your life and focus mainly on the negative aspects.
- You may feel like you want someone to rescue you and solve your problems for you. You feel like you need someone else to make you feel better or change your state of mind.

Listen, I get it. Sometimes you are going to feel weak and helpless and want someone to come to your pity party and tell you it's not your fault and everything is going to get better. You want them to cheer you up.

But, if you are finding yourself moaning and complaining, acting like the world is working against you often, you are setting yourself up for a life with no power to manifest what you want.

If you've identified you tend to take a little too much comfort in any of the above mindsets, it's time to ask yourself one very critical question: What benefits am I getting from having a victim mentality?

For every behavior, there are costs and benefits. It's time you understood yourself a little better and figure out what benefits you receive when acting in a certain way. This will help you understand if you operate with a victim's mentality. If you do, next you need to find ways to fulfill those needs in a more responsible, healthier way which puts you back in charge of your life.

Victim Exercise:

Step 1: Recall a situation in your life where you feel you are a victim.

Step 2: Write down the benefits of being a victim.

Step 3: What needs are being fulfilled by having a victim mentality?

Step 4: What are some healthier ways to get those needs met?

Step 5: What can you do now to begin the process?

Here are the signs you accept responsibility for your current situation and that you take control of your life:

- You are aware of how you've contributed to your own challenges. You can see where you made poor decisions or failed to take action. You can also look at the great parts of your life and give yourself credit for those, as well.
- You remember all the wonderful things you've accomplished and work toward building your self-esteem. Taking responsibility builds self-esteem.
- You know not everything is within your power to change. For example, you can't make people like you. You don't have control over any person, same as they have no control over you. But you can change the circumstances of your life,

so you do not need to interact with them. You can find another job. You can change your relationships. Don't worry about things you cannot change.

- You focus on being the best version of yourself. You hold yourself to a higher standard than anyone else would ever demand of you. This is the ultimate way to take control, because you're accepting the highest level of responsibility. Being the best version of yourself means doing what needs to be done, whether you feel like it or not.

- You avoid blaming yourself. Taking responsibility and taking the blame are very different. Does it matter who's to blame? Just take care of it. Solve the problem creating a roadblock in your life. It doesn't matter whose fault it is. You're going to forge ahead and make your dreams come true.

- Your willingness to get uncomfortable. Why do people avoid responsibility and turn to the victim approach? Because it seems easier and more comfortable than being responsible. Taking responsibility can be uncomfortable. But discomfort is where all the growth happens.

Failure to take responsibility comes at a high price. The biggest costs are a loss of self-respect, feeling as though you lack the ability to change the course of your life, and increasing the likelihood of depression.

When you adopt the responsible mindset, you feel empowered and in control of your life.

Responsible Exercise:

Step 1: Tap back into that situation where you felt like you were a victim. Only this time, change your perspective 180 degrees. Imagine you are responsible and write your new answers.

Step 2: Write down the benefits of being responsible.

Step 3: What needs are being fulfilled by having a responsible mindset?

Step 4: What are some healthy ways you are meeting these needs?

Step 5: What is one action you can take to demonstrate you accept responsibility for the situation?

Remember, response ability! You choose your response every moment of every day, even when it seems like you did not choose a situation. Realize many of your choices are made automatically because of the filters and limiting beliefs in your subconscious mind. You may not have specifically chosen any given situation you're presented with; however, you have made thousands of choices throughout your life, deliberately as well as unconsciously and automatically. It's those choices which ultimately create the results you have now.

Right now, you have a choice to make, one that can change the course of your life. One choice leads to a life of helplessness, neediness, and scarcity. The other will lead to a life of freedom, empowerment, and happiness.

Which choice will you make?

Download *Responsibility Meditation Script* at:
http://www.VictoriaMGallagher.com/ploabook

Section 5: Techniques to Raise Your Vibration

Attraction is a law but it's the secondary law, the primary law is the law of vibration. The law of vibration is one of the basic laws of the universe.

It decrees that everything moves, nothing rests, we literally live in an ocean of motion.

- Bob Proctor

Technique #1 Goal Setting

SMART goals help you narrow your focus, so that you can become crystal clear as to exactly what you want. Remember the Law of Attraction brings to you what you think about, so you never want to use negative words, only positive ones. In other words, you always want to focus on what you want, rather than what you don't want.

In case you're not familiar with a SMART goal yet, SMART is an acronym and I have tailored it a bit to be a bit more Law of Attraction oriented:

- Specific
- Measurable
- Aligned
- Realistic
- Timetable

Let's look at the process of creating a SMART goal now.

Choose an Area of Focus:

Once you determine what issue you want to focus on, you can then begin to identify exactly what result you want to create in that area.

The process you will go through to get very specific is the SMART goal setting technique that will help you make sure that your goal has certain criteria to not only demand that you be more specific, but it is also used as a measuring stick, so you will know when you have achieved it.

The area of Focus for this SMART goal will be RELATIONSHIP.

SMART Goal Creation

SPECIFIC:

It's important to articulate exactly how you want to see the situation, so in creating a specific goal for love, we always want to ask ourselves exactly what we are looking for. Saying something like, *"I want to be in a great relationship"* is not clear enough, because we are in relationships with many kinds of people already like friends, business associates etc. First, we must look at what we are looking for. It would be more appropriate to say something like this instead:

Example: *"I want a partner who is committed, romantic, honest, trustworthy, attractive, loving, passionate and kind."* This is very specific.

MEASURABLE:

Let's make it measurable now.

How will you know you have achieved your goal? This needs to be defined very clearly. What is the one detail that can be measured? If it's a weight goal, that's easy, how much do you want to weigh. If it's a money goal, how much money?

Using our relationship goal example: You can measure that as well by stating what stage of the relationship you will be in.

Some examples would include: Exclusively dating, engaged, married?

ALIGNMENT:

Go deep here and check in with your intuitive self, to make sure you desire this thing deeply and why?

Are your goals aligned with your purpose? The more your goals are aligned with your purpose, the more effortlessly you'll achieve them.

If your goals are not in alignment with your desires, beliefs, and thoughts, there will be a lot of resistance. Would you enjoy the actions you need to take?

Does it match up with your beliefs? Does it conflict with other goals you are working on? Are you willing to do the inner work to release the beliefs that are not in alignment with this goal?

Example: With the relationship goal you might ask: *Do I want to be married, or is it because it's what everyone else thinks I should do?*

Do I have time in my life to dedicate to the kind of relationship I want?

This is a yes or no response to whatever questions you need to consider.

REALISTIC:

Ask yourself, do I believe I can achieve this? If not, you might want to start with a smaller chunk of what you want at first. Or maybe you can push the timeline out to a more realistic date.

Example: If you believe it's realistic, then that's a simple *yes!*

TIMELINE:

Putting a timeline on your goals is an integral part of the process. A goal without a timeline is simply a dream. A timeline is what turns the goal into a commitment and you are much more likely to achieve it, even if it's not by the actual date. It is interesting however, that the subconscious mind tends to set up the conditions necessary to help you achieve it at or very near the timeline you set.

Just don't get too attached to this date, because that will create stress and anxiety and have the opposite effect.

Set a reasonable date in the future that you will achieve it. If you think it will take one year, rather than saying one year, state the date on the calendar instead. The future date is a much clearer instruction to the subconscious mind, rather than a year from now. Because every time you see *"a year from now"* you are pushing it out further and further.

I invite you to consider the wise words from Tony Robbins when coming up with a reasonable timeframe:

> *"Most people overestimate what they can do in a year and underestimate what they can do in two or three decades."*

To ensure that your timeline is accurate, start at the end and work backwards.

Build out your timeline with checkpoints at say the 6-month mark, the 3-month mark, the one-month mark, etc.

Example Timeline: *"I expect to be married within 3 years. Engaged within 2 years. Exclusively dating within 9 months. Meet my soulmate within 6 months."*

Download *S.M.A.R.T. Goal* Worksheet at:
http://www.VictoriaMGallagher.com/ploabook

Technique #2 Affirmations

Create Your Own Powerful Affirmations

When creating affirmations, it is important to narrow down your focus to one area of your life. Trying to work on too much at once can overwhelm the subconscious mind. Taking the time to home in on the most pressing issue as discussed in the previous chapter on Goal Setting is the first step.

Let's now turn these SMART goals into SMART affirmations.

The next step of this process, now that you have a clear goal you are committed to and focused on, it's time to create smart affirmations that support you.

Here are some Key Points in creating your affirmations:

- **Keep it positive:** They need to be focused on what you do want, not on what you don't want.

In other words, do not include any words that give attention to what you are trying to get away from. If you are trying to stop attracting bad relationships, you don't want to say anything like, *"I no longer attract bad relationships."* Instead, you'll state something which resonates with an aspect of your SMART goal, *"I am ready to attract a loving and committed relationship."*

- **Make it believable:** The goal of affirmations is simply to help you feel the good feelings. It never feels good when we lie to ourselves, so do not make affirmations that are lies, otherwise they will be rejected by your subconscious. Example: *"I am now in the relationship of my dreams."* Are you really? If that is not true, no amount of repeating it is going to get you to believe it. You feel awkward when you say it. It doesn't feel good because you're lying to yourself and your subconscious mind knows it.

What's a truthful part of that statement you can believe right now? Reword using opening statements like, *"I am choosing to," "I am willing to," "I am creating," "I allow," "I am ready to experience," "I invite," "I am open to," "I deserve,"* etc.

I now invite a loving relationship into my life.

I take daily action toward attracting my dream partner.

I am ready to experience romance.

I now allow myself to feel attractive

I choose to believe my soulmate is looking for me.

- **Be concise:** The quicker you can say them, the better. Keep your affirmations short, memorable, sound bites. The easier they are to remember and say, the better chance they have at influencing the subconscious mind.

- **Use present tense:** Rather than saying things like, I will have, or I am going to have, or I want, say what is happening in this moment that is true about it. A good rule of thumb is to make it about a feeling that you can experience in the present. You could say, *"Every day, I am welcoming more and more love into my life,"* *"I'm excited about meeting my soulmate,"* or *"I am worthy of enjoying a committed relationship."*
- **Use *"I am"* statements.** I and am are the two most powerful words. What follows *"I am"* starts the creation of it as your subconscious mind will immediately go to work if you truly believe in your statements.

Here are Ten Affirmations that Support the Above SMART Relationship Goal:

1. I invite love into my life.
2. I am ready for a committed loving relationship.
3. I am creating space in my life for a loving partner.
4. I deserve to be part of a loving, intimate relationship.
5. I am attractive and loveable.
6. I am worthy of great love.
7. I am well-aware that I have much to offer in a love relationship.
8. I am a wonderful, loving person.
9. I am excited about being in a new relationship.
10. I am ready to be part of a loving, committed relationship with a partner who is honest, trustworthy, attractive, passionate and kind.

Now that you have your list, always keep it handy. Read your affirmations out-loud at least twice per day. Once every night before you go to bed, and every morning when you first wake up. Say them with feeling, as if you already are in possession of the desired outcome. Use them in your self-hypnosis, (upcoming chapter). Keep repeating them to yourself when you're walking, exercising, driving, or any other repetitive tasks.

Technique #3 Self-hypnosis

Self-hypnosis, also known as auto-suggestion, is a self-induced state of deep relaxation where suggestions can be accepted by your subconscious mind.

It is easy to learn self-hypnosis and, as with everything else in life, practice makes perfect!

I want to share with you a very easy way to remember how to put yourself into a self-hypnosis state.

You are Going to Learn How to:

- Induce a deeply relaxed state.
- Give yourself the suggestions.
- Trance termination.

Here's What you Should Expect.

Everyone can be hypnotized, although no two people will experience trance in the same way. So, don't expect your experience to be the same as someone else's!

Also, depending on your state of mind, you may experience something completely different from one day to the next. It's best not to judge or expect it to always be the same.

The hypnotic state is a state you've already experienced many times throughout your life. It may not feel quite as mysterious and enchanting as you might expect.

Here are a Few Signs that you are in a Trance:

- Breathing and pulse rate slow down.
- Tingling or numbness in your fingertips.
- A light feeling like you are floating.
- A heavy feeling like you are sinking.
- Fluttering eyelids.

Some people are naturally more suggestible than others.

If you would like to determine your suggestibility, you can visit the resources page at:

http://www.VictoriaMGallagher.com/ploabook

In hypnosis, you are always in control, and always aware of your surroundings and you can come out of it any time you like.

It feels very much like daydreaming, like those times when you find yourself zoning out. You pass through this state as you wake up and when entering sleep.

Although your body appears to be asleep, your mind is extremely focused, aware, and attentive the whole time. It's best to remain slightly awake, so that you can perform the inner work.

Your attitude is the key to successful self-hypnosis.

No one can be hypnotized against their will. If you approach hypnosis with the intention to prove that you cannot be hypnotized, then you simply will not enter the state.

If you use hypnosis with an open mind, then the possibilities are limitless.

Before you begin, set an intention for the session.

Bring your list of affirmations you created in the previous chapter. It would be a good idea for you to memorize them if possible so that you won't need to open your eyes and look at your list.

For best results, set aside a regular time to practice self-hypnosis every day. Give yourself a good 20 to 30 minutes every time you practice. Make sure you will not be disturbed and that your environment is quiet.

The Simple 3 – 10 Self-Hypnosis Process:

Step 1: Relax the Body – 5-10 minutes

- Close your eyes.
- Take **10** slow and deep diaphragmic breaths.

- Relax **10** areas of your body by placing your awareness on each area and visualizing each part of your body relaxing.

Head, Neck, Shoulders, Arms, Hands, Chest, Stomach, Buttocks, Legs, Feet.

Step 2: Relax the Mind 5 minutes

Deepen your relaxation by very slowly counting backward **10 – 1**. Imagine yourself walking down a set of **10** stairs. Between each number, say to yourself, *"I am relaxing deeper and deeper. Down. Down. Down."*

Step 3: Inner Work 10 minutes

- **VISUALIZE/FEEL** – 3 – 5 minutes

Imagine yourself with your desired outcome. **FEEL** the emotions as much as possible.

- **AFFIRM/FEEL** – 3 – 5 minutes

Repeat your affirmations. **FEEL** the emotions as much as possible.

Step 4: Trance Termination - 1 – 3 minutes

Simply say to yourself, *"I will now return to full waking consciousness at the count of three and feel fully refreshed and revitalized."* Then slowly count, *"1. 2. 3. Wide awake and my eyes are now open! I feel great!"*

Download 3-10 Self-Hypnosis Script at: http://www.victoriamgallagher.com/ploabook

If you want to take your self-hypnosis skills to the next level, then take my **free 8 Day Self-Hypnosis Video Training Course at:**

https://www.VictoriaMGallagher.com/learn-hypnosis

Technique #4 Meditation

What's the difference between Meditation and Self-Hypnosis?

In the simplest terms, meditation and hypnosis are similar states of mind, with two different intentions.

The intention in hypnosis is about embedding new suggestions into your subconscious mind.

The intention in meditation is about noticing what is already there.

In meditation, you're not clearing your mind, so much as you are just noticing thoughts and letting them pass by without becoming attached to any thought.

The approach to get into meditation is similar in that you are going to relax your mind and relax your body.

Your meditation begins the moment you sit down and intend to meditate. There are many different techniques. Some you'll focus on a word; called a Mantra, such as *"I am," "calm,"* or *"peace."*

Or you might meditate by becoming aware of your breathing, not trying to alter it in any way, but just observing it at various places on your body.

To clear up any confusion, there is also guided meditation, and quite frankly, there is not too much of a difference between guided meditation and self-hypnosis.

For our purposes, I'll be teaching you the technique of meditation from a more traditional standpoint.

The technique I would like to share with you is one that I learned while attending a **10-Day Vipassana Meditation Retreat**.

Vipassana Meditation

Vipassana means to come and see or to look inward.

The Vipassana breathing technique simply means to watch the breath with awareness.

This meditation asks us to simply breathe in our own natural rhythm, nothing more and nothing less.

For this meditation, set a timer on your phone. There are also many amazing apps out there, one that I use is called **Insight Timer**.

If you have never meditated before, start with 5 minutes and work your way up over time.

For best results, work your way toward a consistent twice daily meditation practice and spend anywhere from 20 minutes to 1 hour during each session.

Sit either Indian-style on a floor, cushion, pillow, or mat. You want your spine to be straight. You may also do this while seated in a chair if the floor is too uncomfortable. You'll want to still try to support your own spine and keep your feet flat on the floor.

You'll begin by closing your eyes and placing all your attention on the area around your nostrils.

Notice the sensations in that area as you continue to breathe, without forcing or manipulating it in any way. Simply observing the natural breath.

As thoughts come and go, acknowledge them, and let them float away.

In a nut shell, that is the entire process. You will simply observe respiration in that one very focused area the entire time and continue putting your focus on that area every time your mind slips away and starts thinking.

Observe without judgment.

Simply be aware of the physical sensation of your breath, particularly as you breathe in through the nose and out through the nose.

Do not judge yourself when your mind runs away, because it will.

This exercise helps you in so many ways, including non-judgement, controlling your mind, and detaching.

After a few sessions of this, you will have gained some proficiency within the nostril area.

To advance to the next level with this meditation, you will expand your awareness to the rest of the body slowly placing your attention on each area starting at the top of your head and moving down to the tips of the toes.

Again, you are only to observe, not judge, sensations. If you feel pain, allow it. If you feel wonderful sensations, don't become too attached to them. What you will notice is sensations come and go. A fundamental law of nature is change. Lack of understanding this law is the main cause of suffering.

The purpose of this exercise is to release your attachments and become equanimous.

The feelings of need and attachment can block manifesting. The more your happiness depends on a result, the more you repel that result.

Practicing Vipassana meditation daily will help you release your neediness about the outcomes you desire, bringing you peace of mind, which is about the best feeling and highest vibration you can experience.

Technique #5 Prepare to Receive

Create room in your life. Make all the necessary arrangements. Otherwise, the universe does have a way of bulldozing in and making room for you!

You need to have faith! If you could already see everything happening, you wouldn't need to have any faith. When you can't see anything has manifested itself yet and still act as though it has, you know you are expecting the universe has heard your intention.

You are putting actions behind your belief—and the universe pays attention to this! On a more practical level, it's also sending suggestions to your subconscious mind that this is happening, and it had best get on board with the program. That's what causes your subconscious mind to begin working with the supernatural forces in your favor.

This is an action step you need to take now. You've intended for your desire to come, you've visualized, spoken to the subconscious, you've released limiting beliefs, and now you are in a place where you are expecting. When you expect something to happen you prepare. If you expect to move, you begin packing. If you expect to meet the man or woman of your dreams, you create closet and cabinet space for their arrival. If you expect to go into business for yourself, you get a business license. If you expect to land a job that requires you to wear a certain type of clothing, you buy the clothes.

Exercise to Increase Positive Expectancy:

Step 1: Write down at least three positive things you expect yourself to achieve each day.

Step 2: Change something that illustrates you are preparing for your ultimate desire to manifest.

Download *Positive Expectancy* Worksheet at:
http://www.VictoriaMGallagher.com/ploabook

Technique #6 Gratitude

You have so much to be thankful for, if you look.

So many people in this world go without basic needs: food, shelter, or clean water. Many people struggle just to get by each day. They may not even have a place to live.

Right now, you can choose to change your perspective from focusing on what you don't yet have, to realizing how blessed you are to have these gifts. They are gifts worthy of your gratitude.

Walk around the place you live. There are plenty of things right with it. You might also find ways to improve the things you don't like about it to better meet your present needs.

Take a few moments each day to remind yourself of your many blessings. Think of the people who love you. Take a moment to mentally send them love and gratitude.

Remember all the ways in which life is easy for you. Think about the gifts and talents you have to share.

Recognize how easily certain things do come to you.

Sure, some things are more challenging and come less easily. What opportunities are there for you to learn?

Yes, I am saying you can even be grateful for the challenges.

Take time to be conscious of each blessing. When you become aware of all the abundance surrounding you, and feel full of gratitude, you'll attract more abundance to be grateful for.

Everything in your life is there because you attracted it.

Simply acknowledge its presence, find something about each circumstance or person to be thankful or grateful for, and then move on. Acceptance and acknowledgment are the key here. Resisting what you don't like or want only increases its presence.

Positive feelings are associated with greater creativity, increased problem-solving ability, and greater overall success in life.

Gratitude Exercise

Taking the time to do a simple exercise like this every day helps you refocus your thoughts. When you are constantly worrying about things you don't have or things that haven't yet happened, you might forget to consider all the wonderful things you do have.

It's time to close your eyes for a moment and think of at least 10 things you are grateful for right now. If you find it difficult to get started, here are some suggestions:

- I am grateful for my family.

- I am grateful I had a good breakfast.

- I am grateful that I have great friends.

- I am grateful that I have a warm bed to sleep in.
- I am grateful for this beautiful place where I live.
- I am grateful for the work I get to do.
- I am grateful for my wonderful spouse.
- I am grateful for my lungs.
- I am grateful for my cat.
- I am grateful for technology.

Gratitude Assignment

It doesn't matter how small some of these might feel, just be grateful for what you are blessed with, no matter what.

Close your eyes for 10 minutes and experience being present in the moment. Get a sense of all the gifts you have in your life. Send appreciation to each one.

Open your eyes and write down at least 10 things you are grateful for.

Download *Gratitude* **Worksheet at:**
http://www.VictoriaMGallagher.com/ploabook

Technique #7 Practice Self-love

Your relationship with yourself is the most important connection you'll ever have. Still, it can be hard to remember to express love and compassion to yourself.

What does it mean to love yourself?

How you feel about yourself influences all your experiences, as well as all your relationships with others.

Loving yourself is accepting yourself, right now, as you are. It exists even when there may be things about yourself you wish you could change.

It does not mean you are arrogant or conceited, or you feel you are better than anyone else. As a matter of fact, judging and comparing oneself to another is one of the worse things you can do to your self-esteem. Once you start playing the judgment and comparison game, you'll quickly realize there is always someone else you'll secretly feel is better than you. It's best not to compare yourself with anyone.

You are a unique human being and there is no one else in the world exactly like you. Seek to discover what makes you unique.

No one is perfect. We all have strengths and weaknesses. Luckily, as you invest in and work on your personal growth—as you are now doing—you will develop the capability to build on your strengths. You can also improve any perceived weaknesses. These actions help you to become the best version of yourself.

Respect yourself. Take care of yourself physically, mentally, and emotionally. Have pride in your appearance. Know your limits and define what behaviors you consider acceptable.

Realize you are a worthy human being. You are worthy of love. Until you love yourself, you will not be able to love anyone else. You can only love another to the degree you do yourself.

Self-Love Exercise

Give yourself a boost of self-love.

Start by creating a list of all your positive qualities.

What do you love about yourself?

Use this list as a guideline and list at least 10 positive qualities in each area:

- Your body
- Your mind
- Your personality
- Your physical abilities
- Your talents

Take this list and place it where you can see it. Read it out loud every day.

Download *Self-Love* Worksheet at:
http://www.VictoriaMGallagher.com/ploabook

.

When it Doesn't Work

How long should you try? Until.

` Jim Rohn

Giving up on yourself so soon? The Law of Attraction doesn't always conform to your exact timeline.

Listen, I so badly want you to have your dreams and your goals. However, you've got to want them bad enough (without being anxious and clingy!) to stick with it! That's the part I can't do for you. No one can, except you.

Here's the thing about this very thought of it not working. If you've been counting down the days until you can quit trying to make Law of attraction work, then there are a few things to consider.

- Realize, thinking *"Law of Attraction isn't working"* is a self-limiting belief and not in alignment with manifesting.

- The work you are doing, should be enjoyable so that you're in the moment. You're happily pursuing your passion. You're not concerned about how much longer it's going to take.

- Practicing Law of Attraction is a lifestyle change. It's not just something you do temporarily. It's a way of life.

- You've got to have a desire that is worthy of you. If you're so quick to give up on it, why?

- How bad do you want it? Do you want it as bad as a prisoner wants to escape from prison?

In a sense, you are in prison right now. Truly, if you have any idea how powerful you are, you would be free.

Do you have a better way to break free of self-limitations? All the practical steps you need to take to manifest your desires are right here in this book. It's up to you now to do the necessary work on yourself.

Create Your Law of Attraction Success Plan

Congratulations! You've just completed reading the book and now you're ready to apply what you've learned in the most practical and effective way.

To reiterate, manifesting happens when there is alignment between all eight conditions. Where you begin your unique journey, and the inner work you need to do, depends on how well you are already aligned with each of the conditions.

There are limitless approaches to working with the exercises.

Regardless of which path you take, realize that you are raising your energy vibration just by your very commitment to doing consistent daily inner work on yourself. For some people, a minimal approach can have very favorable results.

The very first thing you should do is the **14 Day Set Up**.

The **14-Day Set Up** is to be used as a guideline to create the groundwork for your daily manifesting routines. You can use this schedule or go at your own pace. After you have read the book one time through, begin again at Section 3: **The Conditions**. The **14-Day Set Up** is the process you go through one-time, where you'll create your personalized manifesting resources which you'll be using during your daily and weekly routines.

During this time, you'll also begin one daily routine of reading your **Desire, Intention, and Gratitude Statement**, which you'll create on Days 1 and 2.

Download your 14 Day Set Up guide at:
http://www.VictoriaMGallagher.com/ploabook

Then, after you have completed the **14-Day Set Up**, you'll begin your daily manifesting routines.

Here are a few suggested methods for daily manifesting.

Method 1: One Condition at a Time

One way to get yourself started would be to simply begin with the exercises in the desire chapter. Then move through each chapter at your own pace, focusing daily, only on that one chapter, over a period time until you feel complete in that area. That might mean 7 days, or it could mean 60 days. Then, move on to the next chapter and repeat.

Method 2: Alternate Conditions Daily

Another approach would be to rotate through each of the conditioning exercises daily. Day one, Desire statement. Day two, Focus Meditation, Day three, Visualization, etc. and then go back to day one.

Method 3: Several Conditions at a Time

Here's a method where you could incorporate several, if not all, of the techniques into your daily routine.

Commit to perform a few, if not all the conditioning exercises daily. Set up a daily routine that you can be consistent with. For example, for a period of 30 days, you could focus on your limiting beliefs, focus meditation, desire and intention statement, and daily affirmations.

Then, in another 30-day round, you can change the routine and concentrate more on improving visualization, take daily action, celebrate your manifestations, and improve one of the qualities from section 4, using the included meditation.

The first step is to take some time now to determine how much time in each day you will dedicate to your development.

When you choose how much time to commit to the inner work, consider this: Training your mind and your emotions takes effort. However, it is the most important thing in life. Even if you lost your health, which is the next most important thing, your mind could help you get it back.

If you are consistent, you will be able to make major improvements in your life, and in your manifesting power. Law of Attraction teachers Esther and Jerry Hicks often talk about how one hour spent on your inner journey has the same impact as seven hours of taking action in the outer world.

You can create your own routine, using the worksheet I provide. Or you can choose one of the 3 sample routines I put together for you, that you can commit to daily for a minimum 90 days. Why 90 days? Do I have to do this every day? You've probably heard that it takes 21 days to change a habit. The truth is it can take anywhere from 2 months to 8 months to truly change a behavior. Also, if you're not willing to put in a minimum of 60 minutes a day to change your life, then you probably don't have a burning desire that is strong enough yet.

Fortunately, the more you work with getting into alignment with the manifesting conditions, the better you will feel, so this will be enjoyable. This is a lifestyle you are creating, not another self-help book you read one-time and did not apply. Application is everything when it comes to the Law of Attraction.

Also, when you pair everything with the self-hypnosis scripts and audio recordings found in the members area, change will happen much more rapidly.

Choose your ideal level of participation:

Level 1: "I'm Feeling It! I could be into this!"

Daily Commitment: 60 minutes

You know you need Law of Attraction in your life, but you're just way too busy to make a lot of time for it. So, you're willing to take it slow and steady, realizing results may take longer.

Daily Routine:

- D.I.G. Statement 10x Day - 10 Min
- Meditation to Focus Your Mind - 10 Min
- The Visualization Process - 5 Min
- New Belief - Self-Hypnosis - 25 Min
- Technique #4 Meditation - 10 Min

Weekly Routine:

- The Laboratory in Your Mind - 20 Mins
- Inspired Action - 10 Mins
- Action by Giving - 10 Mins
- Celebrate your Manifestations - 5 Mins

Level 2: "I'm Fired Up! Let's do this!"

Daily Commitment: 90 minutes

You're ready for change and you want to give it a good go. You'd like to check it out and if you don't get results in 30 days, you're outta here, right? Slow down, horsey. Remember, one key to success is that you need to do something different. How about committing to this plan for the next 90-days and report back to me the difference you have made in your life?

Daily Routine:

- D.I.G. Statement 10x Day - 10 Min
- Meditation to Focus Your Mind - 15 Min
- The Visualization Process - 10 Min
- New Belief - Self-Hypnosis - 25 Min
- Technique #4 Meditation - 15 Min
- Celebrate your Manifestations - 5 Mins

Weekly Routine:

- The Laboratory in Your Mind - 20 Mins
- Inspired Action - 10 Mins
- Action by Giving - 10 Mins

Level 3: "Full-on Fast Track! - I'm All In! Bring it!"

Daily Commitment: 120 minutes

You're a Law of Attraction go getter! You are excited, committed, ready to take massive action, speed things up, and get yourself lined up with the manifesting conditions now!

Daily Routine:

- D.I.G. Statement 10x Day - 10 Min

- Meditation to Focus Your Mind - 20 Min
- The Visualization Process - 15 Min
- New Belief - Self-Hypnosis - 25 Min
- Technique #4 Meditation - 20 Min
- Celebrate your Manifestations - 5 Mins
- Inspired Action - 10 Mins
- Action by Giving - 10 Mins

Weekly Routine:

- The Laboratory in Your Mind - 20 Mins

Do the routine of your choosing every day consistently for 30 days.

Then, to kick your vibration up a notch, add on or swap out one of the rituals and begin working through each of the manifesting qualities from section 4. There is a meditation script provided for each one.

Simply choose one of the qualities to focus on for 30 days and record yourself reading one of my meditation scripts or download my pre-recorded one from the VIP members area.

Download Daily Routine Worksheet at:
https://VictoriaMGallagher.com/ploabook

Time is Now - Live it!

Your life is about to transform in the most profound way and I am excited for you!

Now you have a better understanding of how the Law of Attraction works. Each day from now on, you can create your ideal life exactly the way you design.

As you begin this journey, determine what it is you want. Imagine all the possibilities your world could now include as you truly embrace all that you are.

The power is within you and has been there all along.

This is your life. Think of those things you've always loved to do and how you can start doing them!

Life was meant to be enjoyed. You get to choose who you want to be and do whatever you like to do. You can choose to wake up each day and feel passionate about your life. Feel the good that is waiting for you. You deserve the good life.

Give yourself room to grow and experiment with the exercises.

I believe as more people choose to connect with their deepest desires, align with the manifesting conditions so they can live life happily and fully, they cannot help but to contribute positive to the world and make it a much better place for us all.

Each day, as you continue to do the personal development work, you become a master of the law of attraction.

Believe in your dreams and step into them with faith and determination. It's now fully within your reach.

More Law of Attraction Resources

BOOKS

Atkinson, William W. (first edition 1906) Thought Vibration, Or the Law of Attraction in the Thought World
Cosimo, Inc., 2006

Byrne, Rhonda The Secret: Book 1 of 4; The Power: Book 2 of 4; The Magic: Book 3 of 4; Hero: Book 4 of 4
Atria Publishing Group / Beyond Words Publishing, 2006; 2010; 2012; 2013

Dyer, Wayne W. The Power of Intention: Learning to Co-Create Your World Your Way
Hay House, Inc., 2004

Gawain, Shakti Creative Visualization: Use the Power of Your Imagination to Create What You Want in Your Life
Whatever Pub., 1978

Grout, Pam E-Squared: Nine Do-It Yourself Energy Experiments That Prove Your Thoughts Create Your Reality
Hay House Insights, 2013

Hicks, Jerry and Esther Ask and It Is Given, Learning to Manifest Your Desire (The Teachings of Abraham)
Hay House, Inc., 2005

Hill, Napoleon (first edition 1937) Think and Grow Rich
Renaissance Books, 2001

Lipton, Bruce H. The Biology of Belief – Unleashing the Power of Consciousness, Matter & Miracles
Authors Pub Corp., 2005

Losier, Michael J. (Wellness Central Edition) Law of Attraction: The Science of Attracting More of What You Want and Less of What You Don't
Hachette Book Group USA, Inc., 2007

Murphy, Joseph The Power of Your Subconscious Mind
Prentice Hall Press, 2011

Sincero, Jen You Are a Badass at Making Money: Master the Mindset of Wealth

Viking Penguin, 2017

Wattles, Wallace D. The Science of Getting Rich: The Proven Mental Program to a Life of Wealth
Penguin Publishing Group, 2007

MOVIES

The Secret Dir. Drew Heriot. By Rhonda Byrne. Perf. Bob Proctor, Joe Vitale and John Assaraf.
Released by Prime Time Productions, 2006

WEBSITES

Daniels, Elizabeth. "Apply the Law of Attraction." Apply the Law of Attraction, Well Read Gnome, LLC, 2012, www.applythelawofattraction.com/.

Hurst, Katherine. "Discover How to Improve Your Life." The Law Of Attraction, 2018, www.thelawofattraction.com/.

Prout, Sarah. "Official Site." SARAH PROUT, 2018, www.sarahprout.com/.

Vitale, Joe. "Dr. Joe Vitale's Blog." Dr Joe Vitale's Article Database, Hypnotic Marketing Inc., 2016, www.mrfire.com/dr-joe-vitales-blog/.

www.ingramcontent.com/pod-product-compliance
Lightning Source LLC
Chambersburg PA
CBHW060356080526
44583CB00012B/344